Homes and Health

OTHER TITLES FROM E & FN SPON

Unhealthy Housing
Research, Remedies and Reform
R. Burridge and D. Ormandy

Planning and the Heritage
Policy and procedures
M. Ross

Transport Policy and the Environment
D. Bannister and K. Button

Fire from first principles
A design guide for building fire safety
P. Stollard and J. Abrahams

Environmental Planning for Site Development
A.R. Beer

Defects and Deterioration in Buildings
B.A. Richardson

Beazley's Design and Detail of the Space between Buildings
A. and A. Pinder

For more information about these and other titles please contact:
The Promotion Department, E & FN Spon, 2–6 Boundary Row, London,
SE1 8HN
Telephone 071–522 9966

Homes and Health

How housing and health interact

Bernard Ineichen

Department of Public Health and Epidemiology
Charing Cross and Westminster Medical School
University of London, UK

Published by
E & FN Spon, an imprint of Chapman & Hall, 2–6 Boundary Row,
London SE1 8HN

Chapman & Hall, 2–6 Boundary Row, London SE1 8HN, UK

Blackie Academic & Professional, Wester Cleddens Road, Bishopbriggs, Glasgow G64 2NZ, UK

Chapman & Hall Inc., 29 West 35th Street, New York NY 10001, USA

Chapman & Hall Japan, Thomson Publishing Japan, Hirakawacho Nemoto Building, 6F, 1–7–11 Hirakawa-cho, Chiyoda-ku, Tokyo 102, Japan

Chapman & Hall Australia, Thomas Nelson Australia, 102 Dodds Street, South Melbourne, Victoria 3205, Australia

Chapman & Hall India, R. Seshadri, 32 Second Main Road, CIT East, Madras 600 035, India

First edition 1993

© 1993 Bernard Ineichen

Typeset in 10/12 pt Palatino
by Graphicraft Typesetters Ltd, Hong Kong
Printed and bound in Great Britain at the Cambridge University Press

ISBN 0 419 17100 2

A catalogue record for this book is available from the British Library

Library of Congress Cataloging-in-Publication data available

Contents

Acknowledgements

My thanks to the Department of Environmental Health, Royal Borough of Kensington and Chelsea for supplying some of the illustrations

The legacy of the past   1

1.1 BEFORE WORLD WAR I

A good sewer is far nobler and far holier than the most admired Madonna ever painted.

Ruskin

Discussions of the history of housing in Britain that claim a relevance to modern-day society conventionally begin around the time of the ascent of the young Queen Victoria to the throne in 1837. It was a time of rapid social change. One third of the way through the nineteenth century the British population was growing at a furious pace, and even more dramatically, moving from the status of a rural peasantry to an urban proletariat.

Between the censuses of 1801 and 1851 the population of England and Wales doubled: cities grew at a frightful rate. Birmingham, Liverpool and Leeds more than tripled their populations; Manchester quadrupled; Bradford increased eightfold. Growth continued almost as rapidly during the second half of the century: by 1901 London had over six and a half million inhabitants. Glasgow – described by a Parliamentary Committee in 1840 as a place where 'penury, dirt, misery, drunkenness and crime culminate to a pitch unparalleled in Great Britain' – was probably the dirtiest and unhealthiest of all British cities. Fever was so prevalent and distinctive that foreigners came to study it. It had nearly a million inhabitants, with a population density that exceeded a thousand people an acre in places (Smith, 1974).

Housing in these new settings was almost exclusively ruled by market forces. Rents were determined by simple supply and demand. Landlords could ask for whatever they thought they could get. House building was speculative, profit driven and largely unregulated. Behaviour was unregulated too: the new urban populations arrived without the experience of cooperation needed to bring even an approximation of civilised self-containment and dignity to their cheek-by-jowl existence.

As one commentator has put it, the raw industrial cities into which migrants from rural England and Wales, the Scottish Highlands and Ireland poured were as unprepared to receive them as they were unprepared to live in an urban environment (Rosen, 1973).

Physical conditions in the cities could be dreadful. The smell was sometimes appalling. Doctors visiting Glasgow in 1840 report on one scene they found which tells us not just about the physical conditions but also something about why they endured.

> We entered a dirty low passage like a house door, which led from the street through the first house to a square court immediately behind, which court, with the exception of a narrow path around it leading to another long passage through a second house, was occupied entirely as a dung receptacle of the most disgusting kind. Beyond this court the second passage led to a second square court, occupied in the same way by its dung hill; and from this court there was yet a third passage leading to a third court and a third dungheap. There were no privies or drains there, and dungheaps received all the filth which the swarm of wretched inhabitants could give; and we learnt that a considerable part of the rent of the houses was paid by the produce of the dungheaps.

Such smells were perceived as a major threat to health, 'putrid miasmata' in the medical jargon of the day. The miasma theory, that disease was due to noxious gases being breathed in, was at the forefront of the Victorian public health movement. Concern about noxious environmental influences grew alongside, and gradually became enmeshed with, concern about the housing standards of the 'working class'; in effect the great majority of the urban population. Such concern predated precise scientific understanding of how the major epidemic diseases were transmitted.

In the rural settings from which the new town dwellers had migrated, thanks to fresh air and water, people lived longer and their health was generally considered to be rather better. But their wages were so low that they were barely able to stay alive at all. There was no spare money to pay for house improvements; but in many cases homes were tied to the job, and there was no incentive for employer/landlords to make improvements either. Many labourers' homes were no better than hovels. Contemporary accounts in the 1860s describe large families, even with lodgers, crowded into one-bedroom cottages; whole families ill with fever and lying in the same room as a corpse; of damp walls, saturated floors and smoke-filled rooms. A national enquiry in 1864 found cottage dwellers had less than one third of the air-space required in workhouses, and little over half of that needed in common lodging-houses (Burnett, 1986).

The Poor Law appeared a close and constant reality. One village investigation in 1873 found one in eleven residents were officially paupers, and three-quarters were likely to be so at some stage in their lives. Pressure on domestic space increased with the premature destruction of spare homes due to the enclosure of farm land or to reduce the opportunities of Poor Law claimants.

A *Times* reporter visited Exning, Suffolk in 1874, and gives a vivid, firsthand account of the a dilemmas created by rural housing shortage.

Many cottages have but one bedroom. I visited one such cottage in which father, mother, and six children were compelled to herd together – one a grown-up daughter . . . In another case the woman said they had put the children upstairs, and she and her husband had slept in a bed on the brick floor below until the bottom board of the bed had fallen to pieces from damp, and then they had to go among the children again. The sanitary inspector visits these dwellings occasionally to prevent over-crowding, but the difficulty is for the poor to find other cottages, even when they are inclined to pay more rent. Some of the worst of these cottages belong to small occupiers; some are mortgaged up to the hilt, and the owners often can afford neither to rebuild nor repair. It is a hard thing, again, for the sanitary inspector to pronounce a cottage unfit for human habitation, when no better – perhaps literally no other – can be had for the family.

Source: F. Clifford (1875) *The Agricultural Lockout of 1874*, William Blackwood.

Urban health problems such as malaria and typhus were not unknown in conditions of rural squalor, nor were TB and respiratory illness, for which poor ventilation was to blame. But housing conditions in the towns were considerably worse. At the beginning of the nineteenth century, the farm labourer with normal strength and energy could usually find the land and material to build himself a dwelling, however rudimentary. In the towns half a century later, new arrivals from the countryside had to squeeze themselves and their dependants into a housing stock already bulging with occupants.

Improvement was to be brought about by various methods: the use of legislation (at first on a voluntary basis, later by compulsion) which regulated the building of new houses, improved their environment, and cleared the worst of the slums away; through the design of new dwellings to ensure minimum standards; and by the education of poor people and the regulation of their domestic lives.

These changes did not all progress at the same rate, and at times they worked against one another. The progress of public health legislation has received the most attention from historians, possibly because it is easiest to trace.

1.1.1 LEGISLATING FOR PUBLIC HEALTH

In the earliest years of Victoria's reign, concern over public health issues grew rapidly, fuelled by the escalating costs to public funds that followed epidemics. Edwin Chadwick's *Report on the Sanitary Condition of the Labouring Population of Great Britain* was a notable milestone, published in 1842 and selling 100 000 copies. It was followed by a series of legislative measures – over 40 in the years between 1850 and 1880 – which slowly ameliorated some of the health problems of the poor and established a public health service.

The first Medical Officer of Health was appointed in Liverpool in 1847, and other appointments followed, although they remained discretionary until the Public Health Act of 1872.

Restrictions on new building were initially put into practice on a local basis, as a result of the efforts of individual Medical Officers of Health. However by-laws to prevent the construction of poor quality housing such as 'back-to-backs' were often ignored and it was not until the Housing, Town Planning Act, 1909 that there was a general prohibition. Opposition was based on the facts that whatever the disadvantage, back-to-backs made efficient use of building plots, were cheap to construct (and hence to rent) and for all but the end houses guaranteed at least some form of warmth (Wohl, 1983).

Alongside restrictions on new types of buildings went powers to prosecute landlords who did not maintain their property. Under the Torrens Act, 1868, it became the duty of householders to keep their property in good repair; and if they failed, the local authority could do the job themselves and charge them for it, or close the property down. The Cross Act, 1875 went further by encouraging slum clearance and rebuilding on a large scale. Slowly conditions improved. Taxes on bricks, glass and timber were removed between 1850 and 1866. Sanitation and decent drinking water were gradually provided in the rapidly growing cities. Hitherto, water supplies may have been from standpipes distant from the houses and switched on only briefly during the day, or delivered by water cart at erratic times. Obtaining water was hard work for poor families and often led to quarrels between them. It was also expensive. Many middlemen might be involved; tenants who had paid their rent might stand to lose their supplies if the landlord had not paid his water-rate (Gauldie, 1974, pp. 77–8).

Overcrowding, so crucial to the persistence and spread of many of these conditions, was reduced but slowly: the pace did not quicken till the next century. Overcrowding was seen as a threat to moral as well as physical health: phrases such as 'moral corruption' and 'herded into promiscuity' recur as churchmen and politicians deplore what they find, with adolescents of both sexes sharing bedrooms, children sharing with their parents and adults driven out to spend their free time in pubs. Overcrowding was particularly bad in Scotland, where in 1861 64% of the population lived in one- or two-roomed houses. In Glasgow there was an attempt to deal with it directly: a system of 'ticketing' houses was introduced in 1866, by which the number of residents in any particular house was limited by sanitary inspectors. By the 1880s, one seventh of the city's population came under these rules, but enforcement was difficult (Worsdall, 1989).

The clearance of the worst areas of housing was achieved with some success following the Cross Act. In London 40 acres, responsible for the highest death rates, were cleared, mostly in the late 1870s, and new accommodation provided for over 27 000 people. However, the cost was considerable, both for local ratepayers, and for those rehoused, who found they had to pay considerably higher rents (Wohl, 1977).

The poverty of the new townspeople created what seemed for many decades an impossible trap: unable to pay enough rent to house themselves adequately, in a housing market where it was in nobody's interest to add appreciably to the housing stock, because owners of new houses would never receive sufficient rent to make their investment worthwhile. Various Acts of Parliament between 1855 and 1862 encouraged the creation of working-class housing by commercial companies, financed by cheap loans. But the results were disappointingly meagre. Only towards the end of the century, when sufficient earning power had filtered down to the poorest families, did this situation change, by which time both philanthropists and local authorities were making a contribution to new housing stock. This process took a considerable time. In the earlier part of the century, skilled artisans acquired reasonable standards of housing several decades before unskilled labourers, as case studies in several towns have shown (Chapman, 1971).

There were several reasons why Victorian public health and housing legislation did not immediately benefit those most in need. Much legislation was originally voluntary, and became mandatory only subsequently. It called for local resources which were often provided piecemeal, and sometimes local authorities could promote their own Acts of Parliament which effectively restricted the impact of national measures. This happened in Liverpool, reducing the amount spent on new houses.

Progress in providing adequate working-class housing varied from city to city. Some local political groups were particularly powerful, standing in the way of improvements. Back-to-back housing was forbidden by an Act of Parliament in 1842, yet continued to be built for long after. The local administration in Leeds, hand-in-glove with builders' interests, went on building them until 1937 (Beresford, 1971).

Poverty, housing and health in Liverpool

Outside London and Glasgow, Liverpool was probably the unhealthiest of British towns in the middle of the nineteenth century. In 1843 life expectancy of its citizens was 26, against 37 in London and 45 in Surrey. At one period over half the children were dying before their fifth birthday.

The migration of families escaping from the famine in Ireland added considerably to its problems. It was the most densely populated English city, well over double that of London in 1844, with over 700 people per acre in one group of six enumeration districts.

Large numbers of the population (estimates vary between 28 000 and 39 000 in the late 1830s) lived in cellars. The majority of these had been evicted by 1851 as a result of new legislation which followed from Chadwick's 1842 Report. At the same time, the Council feared the implication of proposed regulations concerning new housing, which would put up building costs considerably. When the Building Regulation Bill, 1842 was introduced, Liverpool was able to gain exclusion, and subsequent housing regulations were governed by rules formulated locally. As a result, little new building took place, and tenants evicted from cellars were forced into already existing overcrowded housing.

Source: Treble (1971); Taylor (1974).

Secondly, much of the legislation merely closed down some options (e.g. the banning of the use of cellars as homes) without providing alternatives. It was not until after 1880 that legislative emphasis shifted from clearing away the worst houses to providing new ones. Measures to improve housing actually made some people homeless. The building of railways reduced urban housing still further. Railway companies were not obliged to place limits on their site clearance operations in towns until 1874, when they were required to give eight weeks' notice before taking possession of working-class houses and to provide alternative accommodation. The regulations were easily evaded and did not succeed in ensuring the provision of alternative homes for the neediest of those displaced. According to one estimate, 76 000 homes were lost to railway building between 1853 and 1901 (Dyos, 1982).

Progress in improving workers' housing conditions in rural areas was if anything even slower. The 1909 Housing Act achieved some progress; in the first three years of its operation, 15 000 properties were improved and 5000 cottages compulsorily closed. But Medical Officers of Health were often reluctant to issue closing orders in areas of housing shortage on the grounds that to reduce further the stock of accommodation would only drive labourers and their families into the towns – or the workhouses. Loans to local authorities sanctioned the building of fewer than ten per cent of the number of cottages pulled down under the Act (Burnett, 1986).

Urban environmental improvements had their costs too: White (1980) describes how when Flower and Dean Street in Whitechapel, a slum area long associated with crime and prostitution, was purchased in 1885 in order to rebuild it as 'philanthropic' dwellings, existing tenants were simply evicted: and one died of exposure.

Thirdly, the new legislation called for the creation of entirely new organizations to perform entirely new tasks. The whole apparatus investigation, the identity and measurement of problems, and the devising and execution of remedial action had to be created from scratch. The gradual growth of public health departments has already been noted and public health education was similarly hesitant. The first course of Public Health lectures took place at St. Thomas's Hospital in 1856 and a Diploma in State Medicine (later to become the Diploma in Public Health) was instituted in Dublin in 1870 and in English cities soon after. All medical officers in large districts had to possess one by 1888, and those in County Councils by 1909. Their staff of 'sanitary inspectors' remained minute – Mile End had one per 105 000 population in 1884 – and the inspectors' training was often rudimentary until very late in the century.

One new activity which became a valuable adjunct to the public health movement arose from the Victorian passion for counting. The Registrar-General's office was founded in 1837, and the appointment of Dr William Farr as Compiler of Abstracts provided the public health lobby with its first reliable statistician to contribute to their campaigns. Farr and his colleagues published figures on mortality and disease. In particular they contrasted the life and disease rates for people in different parts of the country, focusing attention on health differentials between 'good' and 'bad' areas. Variations between places and over time in child mortality (62 per cent of labourers' children died before the age of 5) were especially shocking. Reports from the Poor Law Commissioners and local statistical societies added to the impact. Chadwick's Report was able to draw on all this statistical material, and the expertise which made it possible. Subsequently the ability of the Medical Officers of Health to assemble and publish statistical material was a great force in shaping public awareness and achieving political action. In Wohl's (1977) words

Their emphasis on the moral dangers of overcrowding could not be ignored. . . . and their convinced environmentalism forced men to consider causes other than character for the sorry plight of the urban masses.

Fourthly, countervailing forces within society frequently stood between these new organizations and their stated aims. Many of the new local authorities were made up of landlords, the very people who stood to lose most by innovative public health measures. 'Doctor, the less you do the better we shall like you' was the advice to one newly-appointed Medical Officer of Health (Wohl, 1983, p. 187). Gauldie (1974) lists a whole host of reasons why local authorities were ineffective; self-interest and the corruption of councillors, the complexity of the system of administration, with many different authorities with overlapping functions, possibly leading to rivalry; and ignorance of the cause of problems, and thus inability to suggest remedies, or to judge the likely effectiveness of remedies that were proposed.

Serving as town councillors had little attaction for wealthy merchants; manual workers were excluded by the franchise; the result was that 'for the most part, town government was in the hands of the petty bourgeoisie, the very weakness of whose position in society left them open to the suspicion that their motives were not wholly altruistic'. And of course they needed to keep down the rates to please the voters. Officials were appointed on a yearly basis, making them dependent on councillors for job security. Overcrowding broke the law, but made it easier for landlords to pay their rates. Medical Officers of Health did not receive security of tenure until 1909 (in counties) and 1921 (in districts). Nevertheless, particularly in the latter part of the century, progress was made.

1.1.2 THE REALITY OF VICTORIAN HOUSING

There are plenty of descriptions of what life was like for the urban poor in early Victorian Britain. Among English cities Liverpool was notorious.

Those unable to achieve a house, or part of a house, however overcrowded, had a number of options open to them. Cellars were probably the next best thing for most people. Cellars were appreciated by their residents rather more than by public health campaigners, who felt they were invariably poorly ventilated, leaving their residents vulnerable to infection from foul smells. The occupants, on the other hand, felt that having their own front door gave them privacy, and of course many cellars had been originally intended to be occupied by servants, and were thus largely self-contained (Gauldie, 1974, p. 95).

Common lodging houses catered for those who could not obtain even a cellar. In 1854 there were 10 000 in London alone, with 82 000 residents. Henry Mayhew's visit to one of them is shown below.

Glasgow Corporation created its own 'Model Lodging Houses' in the 1870s, of between 240 and 438 beds each. In 1896 a 'family home' for widows and children was added. By 1902 one per cent of the population was living in the city's common lodging houses. In Whitechapel, East

The lodging-house to which I more particularly allude makes up as many as 84 'bunks,' or beds, for which 2*d*. per night is charged. For this sum the parties lodging there for the night are entitled to the use of the kitchen for the following day. In this a fire is kept all day long, at which they are allowed to cook their food. The kitchen opens at 5 in the morning, and closes at about 11 at night, after which hour no fresh lodger is taken in, and all those who slept in the house the night before, but who have not sufficient money to pay for their bed at that time, are turned out. Strangers who arrive in the course of the day must procure a tin ticket, by paying 2*d*. at the wicket in the office, previously to being allowed to enter the kitchen. The kitchen is about 40 feet long by about 40 wide. The 'bunks' are each about 7 feet long, and 1 foot 10 inches wide, and the grating on which the straw mattress is placed is about 12 inches from the ground. The wooden partitions between the 'bunks' are about 4 feet high. The coverings are a leather or a rug, but leathers are generally preferred. Of these 'bunks' there are five rows, of about 24 deep; two rows being placed head to head, with a gangway between each of such two rows, and the other row against the wall. The average number of persons sleeping in this house of a night is 60. Of these there are generally about 30 pickpockets, 10 street-beggars, a few infirm old people who subsist occasionally upon parish relief and occasionally upon charity, 10 or 15 dock-labourers, about the same number of low and precarious callings, such as the neighbourhood affords, and a few persons who have been in good circumstances, but who have been reduced from a variety of causes. At one time there were as many as 9 persons lodging in this house who subsisted by picking up dogs' dung out of the streets, getting about 5*s*. for every basketful. The earnings of one of these men were known to average 9*s*. per week. There are generally lodging in the house a few bone-grubbers, who pick up bones, rags, iron, etc., out of the streets. Their average earnings are about 1*s*. per day. There are several mud-larks, or youths who go down to the waterside when the tide is out, to see whether any article of value has been left upon the bank of the river.

Source: H. Mayhew (1851) London Labour and the London Poor, p. 575.

London, there were four such houses, with 323 places, in Flower and Dean St. alone, at the turn of the century. All were owned by the same man, James Smith. Another in Thrawl St. nearby, housed another 177. Common lodging houses had a bad reputation. Male residents were casual labourers earning a hand-to-mouth existence. Many of the women were part-time prostitutes. Drunkenness, crime and violence were commonplace (White, 1980). Health care can have been no more than basic, although Butt (1971) notes in Glasgow one positive action to promote good health: in the smallpox epidemics of 1884 and 1897 residents who agreed to be vaccinated were granted a week's free lodging.

At the very bottom of the scale stood the workhouse, always a grim possibility for poor people who had fallen on hard times. The half century up to the outbreak of the First World War was the age of the building of huge institutions; by 1915 the Poor Law provided places for up to a quarter of a million people, many of them in infirmaries or sick wards. The quality of care varied from workhouse to workhouse (Crowther, 1981). Although the Poor Laws were finally repealed in 1929, both the large institutions and common lodging houses endured into the 1930s. Indeed many of the Poor Law buildings have remained in use up to the present day as longstay hospitals or homes for elderly people. Attitudes surrounding them go back to the Poor Law Amendment Act, 1834, which led to regimes which treated the sick punitively, as moral delinquents, and to the fear of consignment to the workhouse as 'one of the most ingrained obsessions of the British working classes' (Webster, 1990).

1.1.3 IMPROVEMENTS IN HOUSING AND HEALTH

Many diseases declined in British cities towards the end of the nineteenth century, and mortality rates fell. The contribution made by government health measures, as against that of rising living, and especially nutritional, standards, and that of philanthropy, in improving health, remains a matter of lively controversy (Lewis, 1991). What about scientific advances? Understanding that the spread of diseases came about through infection by contact or by transmission through air or water-borne germs gradually replaced the 'miasma' theory. Cholera, typhus, and other infections diseases, were eventually distinguished from one another and slowly brought under control.

Cholera Contracted by swallowing water or food which had been infected by the cholera virus, a minute bacillus. Often spread by water contaminated by the excreta of cholera victims, or by flies which hatched in or fed upon the diseased excrement. It spread across Asia to Europe, first reaching Britain in 1831 and causing panic in the population. Victims could die within a few hours of first showing symptoms, but more usually died after several days of suffering violent stomach pains, vomiting, diarrhoea and coma. Major epidemics followed in each decade of the mid-nineteenth century, 62 000 dying in the epidemic of 1848–9. Some sufferers refused to enter hospital, making remedial measures more difficult to achieve. Although the association with poor hygiene was always suspected, the cholera bacillus was not identified until 1883. Meanwhile the public health measures put into action by William Budd and John Snow (notably the removal of a pump handle on a well in Soho, a heavily infected area, in 1854) gave a great impetus to the exponents of epidemiological approaches to the disease.

Typhoid is a bacterial disease spread like cholera by contaminated food and drink, especially by water contaminated by human faeces. Symptoms are listlessness, lack of appetite, high temperature and diarrhoea. It affected all classes in Victorian Britain killing the Prince Consort. The fact that carriers might be immune from symptoms added difficulty to its identification. It has been largely contained in Europe by adequate water supplies and sewerage, although occasional outbreaks occur (Croydon in 1937; Zermatt in 1963).

Typhus is spread mainly by the faeces of body lice, exacerbated in conditions of overcrowding. Micro-organisms (Rickettsia) attack the small blood vessels, especially in the brain and skin. Symptoms are delirium, stupor and a distinctive spotted skin rash. It can be combatted very effectively by improved sanitation, and it declined steadily after being distinguished from typhoid in 1869.

Diarrhoea was a major killer of babies, from a variety of causes.

Tuberculosis The major killer of Victorian times, accounting for a estimated one third of all deaths. Transmitted by infected breath and sputum, and most dangerous to those living and working in overcrowded or poorly ventilated environments. Better personal hygiene and improved milk supplies led to dramatic falls in death rates, although the disease has persisted into the second half of the twentieth century and small pockets remain.

Smallpox Almost 42 000 died in the epidemic of 1837–40, but although an effective vaccine was available, public health measures proved less than fully effective. An Act of 1840 made vaccination available at public expense, but on only a voluntary basis. Compulsory infant vaccination was introduced in 1853, although this was never enforced with complete success. Officially eradicated worldwide in 1979.

Some particular housing changes were of benefit. New houses were eventually added to the stock which were of superior quality and more durable, especially following the Public Health Acts of 1875 and 1890, which created arrangements for the purchase of land and the building of houses by local authorities, although the go-ahead for local authorities to build and rent housing had been given as early as the Shaftesbury Act, 1885 (Wohl, 1977).

Secondly, cheap transport towards the end of the century provided a vital opportunity for artisans and the wealthier of the working class to escape from overcrowded areas to more salubrious suburbs, especially in London.

Thirdly, model schemes and philanthropic developments introduced planned mass housing of a reasonable standard for working-class families. The creation of new communities, often with a Utopian flavour, has been a British tradition since the early eighteenth century. Most early attempts were in rural locations, and those connected specifically with industry tended to be located on suburban green-field sites (Darley, 1978). In poor overcrowded urban sites the need was to rebuild at high density, and this meant multi-storey buildings. Although initially housing relatively few people, especially among the poorest, the presence of such large and imposing buildings as those of the early Peabody Trust schemes directed popular consciousness towards the benefits of better housing generally. Their influence is subject to dispute. They may have hastened the acceptance of state intervention in housing that subsequently took place, although it was been argued that they set back the process of housing reform (Gauldie, 1974).

It is clear that improvements did not spread equally throughout the population. Overcrowding remained most serious in the largest towns, especially Glasgow. Child mortality varied by class and place (see p. 6) as well as over time. Innovations such as public baths did not always reach those in greatest need (Wohl, 1983).

The subjects for whom these new health measures were targetted did not always collaborate fully or enthusiastically with them. The poor were bedevilled by unemployment, and the work that was available was frequently casual and seldom well-paid. Knowledge of elementary hygiene was often lacking. The cost of medicines might inhibit calling in the doctor, especially for a child who was sick. Infanticide was not unknown: an insurance policy might provide an unexpected bonus! Some treatments were drastic. Opium derivatives were widely used to pacify sick or fractious children (Wohl, 1983).

Many questions concerning the influence of housing in the health of nineteenth-century city dwellers remain to be answered. Little has been written, for example, on how health factors influenced access to desired housing types. Ability to pay was of course paramount in providing access to desired types of housing, but subtler influences may also have been at work. Families may have been excluded, for example, from the Rothschild Buildings in East London because of mental illness (White, 1980, p. 96).

The Peabody Trust would not let large families crowd into accommodation they deemed too small for them. Restrictions in the terms of tenancies offered by the philanthropic housing trusts discouraged many, and some were formally barred from tenancies. One group, the costermongers, whose barrows and donkeys excluded them from some 'model development' schemes, found their own champions, such as Baroness Burdett-Coutts, who endowed Columbia Square Buildings, Bethnal Green, in 1862. Here 183 coster families were housed, with their own market hall (Wohl, 1977).

Regulations of the Peabody Trust

1. No applicants for rooms will be entertained unless every member of the applicant's family has been vaccinated or agrees to comply with the Vaccination Act, and further agrees to have every case of infectious disease removed to the proper hospital.
2. The rents will be paid weekly in advance at the superintendant's office, on Monday, from 9 am to 6 pm.
3. No arrears of rent will be allowed.
4. The passages, steps, closets and lavatory windows must be washed every Saturday and swept every morning before 10 o'clock. This must be done by tenants in turn.
5. Washing must be done only in the laundry. Tenants will not be permitted to use the laundries for the washing of any clothes than their own. No clothes shall be hung out.
6. No carpets, mats, etc. can be permitted to be beaten or shaken after 10 o'clock in the morning. Refuse must not be thrown out of the doors or windows.
7. Tenants must pay all costs for the repairs etc. of all windows, keys, grates, and boilers broken or damaged in their rooms.
8. Children will not be allowed to play on the stairs, in the passages, or in the laundries.
9. Dogs must not be kept on the premises.
10. Tenants cannot be allowed to paper, paint or drive nails into the walls.
11. No tenant will be permitted to underlet or keep in lodgers or to keep a shop of any kind.
12. The acceptance of any gratuity by the superintendant or porters from tenants or applicants for rooms will lead to their immediate dismissal.
13. Disorderly and intemperate tenants will receive immediate notice to quit.
14. The gas will be turned off at 11 pm and the outer doors closed

> for the night, but each tenant will be provided with a key to admit him at all hours.
> 15. Tenants are required to report to the superintendant any births, deaths, or infectious diseases occurring in their rooms. Any tenant not complying with this rule will receive notice to quit.
>
> *Source*: Wohl (1977), pp. 159–60.

The line between philanthropy and social control could be difficult to draw. Wohl (1977) quotes a Peabody official that the working-class could be better housed in large blocks, 'where they can be brought together and be under control and care and management, and looked after'. But the big blocks raised fears too: of epidemics (soon disproved), of social segregation, of loss of privacy, and of the lowering effects of the buildings' 'inhuman' or 'barrack-like' appearance.

There were those too who opposed philanthropy on ideological terms. Yet the continuing existence of so many of these blocks as valued homes after a century's use is a vindication of their worth. The author's grandparents were tenants of a Peabody flat throughout the entire first half of this century. According to family lore, it served them well.

Octavia Hill provided homes for poorer tenants than did the philanthropists with their Model Dwellings. Her regime also contained strong elements of social control. She allowed families to rent small homes (one or two rooms) at first, then encouraged them to move again to larger ones at higher rents. Gauldie (1974, p. 216) has speculated about the tenants of properties managed by her and her housing visitors, who were supplied with running water and drains, but expected to keep themselves clean and above all not to fall behind, even for one week, with the rent:

> We cannot know, because they leave no written word, how these tenants felt whose homes were managed and whose rents were collected by these earnest ladies. Did they indeed look up to them as shining examples, did they aspire to model themselves upon their precepts? Or did they resent their interference, clean the front doorstep, pay the rent and swear at the departing bustles?

Not every change was appreciated by all. Better health involved the gradual encroachment of bureaucratic bodies into 'private life' in the cause of improving housing and reducing disease. Public health officials met much opposition as they struggled to exert their authority over domestic life. Even such an apparently obvious benefit as universal schooling was opposed by some, on the grounds that more contact between children led to more illness. The desperate state of health of the nation continued throughout the nineteenth century. Only when over 90% of the young men volunteering to fight in the Boer War were rejected on health grounds was public opinion fully awakened to the need for better homes and better health for all (Wohl, 1983). A genuine attempt to provide solutions had to wait even longer, until the cataclysmic events of 1914 to 1918.

1.2 1914–1945

'If a healthy race is to be reared it can be reared only in healthy homes'
King George V

Edwardian Britain enjoyed growing power with stability at home and expanding prosperity and wealth through the worldwide trading strengths of the Empire. World War I threw these processes into reverse, and set in motion huge changes in the way society worked. Those changes were particularly marked in the way the nation was housed.

Again the poor physical quality of army recruits indicated a need for action to improve the health of the poor, through measures such as better housing. By the Armistice, the authorities were spurred by the discovery that during the war four million working weeks a year had been lost by sickness due to environmental conditions, and by fear of civil unrest on the lines of that experienced in Russia and Germany. The British public had high expectations following victory. As the war ended, the slogan 'houses fit for heroes' gave impetus to government action which resulted in a series of Acts of Parliament throughout the next decade establishing 'council housing', the provision by local authorities of substantial numbers of houses especially designed for renting by 'the working class'.

The first council housing had been created in Liverpool in 1869, but progress had been slow. Only 24 000 houses had been provided before 1914. However, the influential Tudor Walters Report, published in the month the war ended, November 1918, laid down standards of size, quality and density for the building of mass council housing in the next decade. It became a blueprint for the huge expansion of council housing in the immediate post-war years.

> Running to just under 100 pages it was the first comprehensive treatise on the political, technical and practical issues involved in the design of the small house. In the housing debates of 1918–19, its authority was virtually unquestionable. (Nuttgens, 1989, p. 51)

What did the Tudor Walters Report propose? It encouraged high standards of construction; building to last; low density; a social mix of residents and different house-types; and a replacement of long terraces by the design of new estates of short streets, culs-de-sac and small clusters of houses grouped together. Great stress was laid on the value of providing light airy rooms. Very detailed plans were suggested both for the inside and outside of new homes; although imaginative, the Report was not unrealistic or utopian. It was wide-ranging, dealing not just with plans for homes and estates, but also with matters such as labour costs and the provision of public transport.

Its ideas were soon carried into action, giving in Burnett's (1986) words, 'a particular stamp to the character of local authority housing, almost always in low-density suburban estates, which at the time was accepted unquestioningly as the best and natural way of housing the urban working-class'.

The initial attempt to implement the ideals of the Tudor Walters Report and to create mass public housing came the following year through the Addison Act. This asked local authorities to set out a programme of house-building, but rising costs of building (subsequently transferred to the taxpayer) slowed progress. Only a third of the projected half a million houses were built. Subsequently the Chamberlain Act, 1923 and the Wheatley Act, 1924 (all three Acts were named after Ministers of Health) gave further incentives to local authorities to build. The Chamberlain Act offered government subsidies to local authorities, conditional financial support to private builders and local authority mortgages to those who had saved enough to buy their own homes. The Wheatley Act raised subsidies, and guaranteed a long-term housing programme. It was the most successful of the three, producing over half a million homes, nearly all by local authorities.

Yet most post-war housing was created by the private sector. Subsidies on small houses built by private builders were introduced immediately after the war. Of the almost two and a half million new homes built between 1919 and 1934, only one in three were provided by local authorities. In the late 1930s, private enterprise boomed as never before, completing 287 500 houses in 1935. These years also formed the first golden age of owner-occupation, notable for the flourishing of building societies and the creation of endless avenues of suburban semis, which catered for the rapidly expanding classes of white collar workers and skilled artisans. The importance of these new movements came not merely from improvements in physical health that accompanied them but also in the opportunities they provided for the less tangible benefits of security, freedom from landlord control, and the expression of individuality; the place where the 'small man' could express himself. In contrast to the dirt and overcrowding of inner urban areas, suburban living offered space, low densities, gardens and access to the countryside. The emigrant from the city could rejoice in raising his family in clean and humane conditions.

Developers and their agents were keen to include healthy living as one of the selling points of the new suburbia, promoting its 'healthy air' and

Figure 1.1 Early twentieth century semi-detached houses: uniform designs but spacious interiors.

its location 'above the fog belt' (Jackson, 1973). One enthusiastic builder even declared that 'A summer in Feltham has the health value of a trip around the world' (Burnett, 1986). But owner-occupation had its costs: as property values levelled off, mortgagees began to default on their payments, and many disappeared.

This large-scale movement of populations outwards and aspirations upwards remained largely undiscussed by contemporary doctors, architects and sociological writers, and suburban living remains stigmatized by many intellectuals. (For a full discussion see Oliver *et al.*, 1981.) Government intervention revived in the early 1930s, with the growing awareness of the need for slum clearance. Local authorities were asked to provide plans to clear slums, and subsidized for doing so. After problems on the early years associated with the Depression, considerable progress was made, and a quarter of a million slum dwellings replaced. The effect of these changes, when added to the earlier post-war measures, was to produce an expansion of suburban living for working-class families which mirrored that of the predominantly middle-class owner-occupied areas. In the London County Council Becontree

Figure 1.2 Between the wars semis; everyone's favourite but the intellectuals.

Estate alone, the largest planned suburb in the world became home to 90 000 residents.

Who were these new council tenants? Local authorities were obliged to draw up rules to determine priorities in allocation. In the years after World War I, being an ex-serviceman helped considerably. Later in the 1920s, ability to pay the rent featured. Typical post-war council tenants were a family consisting of a man in a steady manual job earning slightly more than the average wage, with a wife and two young children. There were few pensioners. With the enforced movement of families out of the slums in the early 1930s, the poorest families were brought in, many of whom could not pay the going rate of rent; variable rent schemes were introduced.

Such changes had undoubtedly beneficial effects on the health of the population overall, although notable qualifications were highlighted by perceptive researchers. The left-wing publisher, Victor Gollancz, for example, published two important books in the 1930s challenging the prevailing view that material conditions were improving inexorably. A study of council tenants in Stockton in 1927 rehoused in modern dwellings showed a rise in mortality associated with malnutrition arising from the necessity to spend earnings on goods other than food, most specifically on higher rents (M'Gonigle and Kirby, 1936). McNally (1935) focused on the persisting differences in health between areas in 1933: for example, infant mortality was 59 in outer Birmingham, but 81 in the poorer central area of the city. Differences between towns were even more dramatic: 116 in St Helens, but only 32 in Oxford. There were more infant deaths in St Helens from bronchitis and pneumonia than from all causes put together in Oxford. Conditions like tuberculosis, which persisted due to environmental problems such as overcrowding, actually became commoner in some areas in the early 1920s, and huge geographical variations persisted into the 1930s. Stevenson (1977) records also how conditions changed rapidly over time. As an example, at the end of World War I, fewer than one baby in five in the town of Tynemouth was born in a one-room apartment. In the years between the World Wars, this figure went up to one in three, but was reduced to one in 20 by 1938.

Pockets of extreme overcrowding proved enduring, despite the success of slum clearance. Campbell Bunk, 'the worst street in North London', had an average of more than eleven people crammed into each of its houses in 1938 (White, 1986). However, although continuing inequalities in health were deplored by many, the poorest segment of the population continued to receive less than their share of the growing material prosperity, less than their share of housing, and as a result, more than their share of sickness.

1.3 THE LAST 50 YEARS

> For most people owning one's home is a basic and natural desire.
> *Labour Party's Housing Policy Review 1977*

World War II's immediate impact on domestic housing was severe: an almost total cessation of new building, and severe depletion of the housing stock due to aerial bombing. Yet at its end, similar pressures to those at the end of World War I emerged. Those who had made such sacrifices demanded a better life, and this included improvements in housing.

White (1986, pp. 228–35) describes the impact of the war on the overcrowded residents of Campbell Bunk. Many of the men saw the armed forces as a way of escape, and the women entered war work for better wages than they had ever previously earned. Returning home to the Bunk became 'just too much of a comedown' for some ex-soldiers; one third of the houses were empty by 1946.

The returning servicemen also voted a Labour government into power. The new administration put into action programmes of mass building of council housing, much of it on green field sites, and New Towns created in rural locations well away from existing cities.

The New Town Movement had its origins in the very first years of the century in the work of Ebenezer Howard and Raymond Unwin. Relatively little work had been done on putting their ideas into practice, but the devastation of city centres by enemy bombing, and the prospect of increasing car ownership added to postwar idealism, put much new energy into applying them. A New Town Act passed in 1946 led to the eventually creation, over the next 40 years, of 25 New Towns of nearly a quarter of a million houses. Healthy living in low-density settlements on Green Belt land was among their most potent attractions.

Postwar suburban council estates, and the New Towns, became the subjects of major relatively sophisticated epidemiological studies, and were soon shown to have drawbacks as well as advantages. Their apologists stressed the health benefits of clean air and adequate space, as had the builders of pre-war owner-occupied estates. But this time the disadvantages revealed concerned primarily the mental rather than the physical health of residents.

A team from the London School of Hygiene and Tropical Medicine carried out a survey of the recently-built Oxhey estate in Hertfordshire in the early 1950s. They found a higher rate of mental illness by a variety of measures (mental hospital admissions, GP consultations for nearly all psychiatric conditions, and the self-reporting of neurotic symptoms) than the national figures would suggest. The rate for psychiatric out-patient referrals equalled the national rate, yet the researchers felt it should be higher as many cases had gone undetected. It was not possible to attribute such figures precisely to environmental factors: there was some evidence, for example, that stresses were more severe among the most recent arrivals, and that they improved over time (Martin *et al.*, 1957). Other studies have shown similar improvements follow settling down after a move, and these will be discussed in detail in section 2.4.

Mild mental illness is difficult to measure with any precision, but a study of two areas of Croydon attempted to test the idea that suburban living was particularly stressful by contrasting the mental health of residents on a new peripheral estate with those in an older central area, interviewing over 3000 people, and examining the hospital and GP records of 10 per cent of the population in each area. They found few differences between the populations and explained such as they found by non-medical factors such as family size and distance from hospital (Hare and Shaw, 1965).

A smaller, but more closely controlled study, was carried out by Hardman (1965) who contrasted consultation patterns in two areas of Liverpool, separated by Aintree Racecourse. Few people in either area were over 50 years old.

Consultation rates in the recently-settled owner-occupied area (where most families were in Class II or III) were consistently higher than those in the renting area, which had been occupied for nearly 40 years, and where families were mostly Class IV or V. This difference was apparent across the spectrum of different physical diseases, although consultation rates for psychological problems were similar in the two areas.

Hardman suggests the explanation lies in a greater readiness to consult their GP among those, especially families with small children, living on the newer estate, because of their relative insecurity and uncertainty in their new setting, itself a result of weakening kinship ties and their unfamiliarity with the norms appropriate in the new setting. This explanation fails, however, to account for the absence of any excess of overt psychological problems.

The lesson from these studies is that improved housing, even to levels generally accepted as adequate, does not of itself remove all inequalities of health. Poverty – absolute, relative or perceived – continues to contribute to the pattern of illness on suburban housing estates. This is true of mental as well as physical illness, and is discussed further in the section on mental health (section 2.2.8). The presence of other factors such as unemployment means that isolating the influence of housing is sometimes difficult.

In the 1960s much of the interest of both politicians and researchers shifted to the introduction of new pre-constructed building techniques, introduced in great quantities, especially within the council sector. High densities were made possible by building tall, and using industrial methods.

> In the period before 1970 densities persistently increased; storey heights rose very fast, even for family accommodation; design, construction and ultimately safety standards were pared down (despite the raising of standards for internal dwelling facilities in the 1960s); community facilities and open space provision were sacrificed to demands for economy in state programmes; and considerable and growing evidence of tenant resistance to mass housing was ignored. (Dunleavy, 1981, p. 2)

Byrne *et al.* (1986, pp. 26–7) describe the early natural history of the St Cuthberts development in Gateshead, hailed at the time in the local press as an example of new technologically innovative architectural practice, and described by Prime Minister Harold Wilson, on its opening in 1970, as an example of the finest town planning in Europe. But tenants described their dwellings as 'egg boxes' and 'rabbit hutches'; within 18 months more than half wanted to leave, and the major local evening paper condemned the scheme as 'the wrong size, the wrong shape, and in the wrong place'. From then on, Byrne *et al.* conclude, things got even worse, both locally and nationally. The health dimension of housing policy disappeared altogether, and in the interests of political gain and progress slum clearance increasingly involved the destruction of sound and well-loved homes.

(a)

Figure 1.3 The end of the high-rise revolution: (a) high-rise flats are boarded up.

Most recent developments of importance include the further expansion of owner-occupation, including the selling off of a proportion of the council stock, often (but not always) to sitting tenants; a sharp reduction in new council house building, accompanied by the introduction of 'market rents'; the creation of a growing sector provided by housing associations and charitable organizations; and an increasing variety of techniques for organizing the housing circumstances of elderly people. Health consequences of these Changes are seldom clear-cut, and will be discussed later.

However, many areas of concern regarding housing's influence on health remain. In Chapter 2, these concerns are listed and discussed.

It is worth noting at this stage some of the shortcomings of any account of the historical influence of housing on health. First, much discussion centres around the development of the public health movement. The reality of housing for the bulk of the population, especially the poorest, is often more difficult to discover. One aspect of this concerned the growing influence of medical authorities in the private lives of individuals, especially among the poor. As White (1986) has expressed it, there was

(b) demolished

'no end to the number of officials whose job was to tell Campbell Bunk people how to live'.

Secondly, several shortcomings in the research enterprise can be identified.

1. Physical health sciences have their own limitations. The teasing out of cause-and-effect of the major killer diseases of the nineteenth century was seldom straightforward and often lengthy. Similar problems surround our understanding of the mechanisms of some contemporary

(c) replacements planned

conditions, such as AIDS or schizophrenia, and effective methods of cure and prevention are seldom immediately apparent. Research and understanding progress by learning which are the right questions to ask.

2. At least in the past, there were few qualified personnel in positions to conduct useful research or make vital decisions. Medical training has placed relatively little importance on matters of public health;

(d) constructed in their shadow

sociological training is a relatively recent innovation, and its formal contribution to the education of health workers more recent still. Two quotations are apposite, the first from an influential review of council housing, conducted in the 1960s:

> We think it relevant to record that while there are over 150 professional staff in the Ministry of Housing and Local Government concerned with housing construction, there is only one who is concerned with housing management. (Cullingworth *et al.*, 1969, p. 25)

Figure 1.4 Selling off council housing may go with greater freedom of self expression through choice of architectural detail.

In the second, Nuttgens (1989, p. 70) recalls interviewing sociologists for the Housing Research Team at Edinburgh University in the 1950s:

> Most candidates had no suggestions to offer. The most experienced man suggested that we should put up some housing and he would return in 20 years to say what we had done wrong.

3. While much survey material is now available, often of a high quality, some aspects of housing experience and behaviour have remained relatively unresearched. For example, we know little of people's attitudes and expectations concerning housing. Satisfaction with housing is not an easy variable to measure, as for many people criticism of their homes suggests they are themselves personal failures. Also we know little of particular groups such as those families who bought their homes from their private landlords as sitting tenants, or families which have moved away from, rather than into, particular housing types. This is especially true of private tenants in the first half of the century, when moving house was extremely common. Often rents and bills were left unpaid. V.S. Pritchett called his first volume of

autobiography *A Cab at the Door* (1968) in remembrance of his parents' succession of 'moonlight flits'. A popular music hall song sung by Marie Lloyd, 'My old man said follow the van', celebrated this event. The health consequences of losing a council tenancy, or an owner-occupied house, more common in recent years, are likely to be even more serious. The appearance and subsequent (belated) destruction of tens of thousands of factory-built bungalows ('pre-fabs') in the years following the end of World War II has passed without any apparent study of their impact on health, although many lasted a quarter of a century, far longer than their designers anticipated. Some 125 000 were built, and they appear to have been very popular with their occupants. One of the last surviving estates, in Catford, South London, has been handed over to self-government by a Tenants Management Cooperative by Lewisham Council 45 years after it was built.

4. In recent years, a growing area of concern has been housing's influence on emotional or mental rather than physical health. Much modern housing is widely considered to be bleak; it does little to fire the imagination of its inhabitants other than by stimulating a desire to move. Such sentiments are notoriously difficult to pin down and measure by conventional research techniques.

5. Much continuing concern is to do with enduring inequalities and relative rather than absolute influences on health. Housing can be viewed as just one element of inequality which permeates modern British society (Morris and Winn, 1990). The consequences for health of housing inequalities will be discussed in a later section. Here, it is sufficient to note how persistent and hard to eradicate have been the old attitudes towards the poor which go back to the nineteenth century Poor Law and the workhouse. Even the creation of a universal, free National Health Service in 1948 has not been enough. The most graphic illustrations have been the series of scandals, revealing gruesome conditions in mental handicap hospitals (whose residents have regarded them as home for up to 70 years). Such dreadful problems of abuse persisted up to the 1970s.

1.4 AROUND THE WORLD

A combination of rising prosperity, greater equality of wealth and access to health care, and aggressive public health initiatives, have combined to make many of the most dangerous diseases of the nineteenth century little more than dreadful memories throughout the industrialized world. Smallpox has been wiped out; cholera, typhoid, typhus, and diseases contracted from rats are now absent or extremely rare in cities in rich countries. Infant deaths have been dramatically reduced. Adequate, healthy housing for the mass of the working-class population has been achieved, to a greater or lesser degree throughout the developed world.

The process has been broadly similar to Britain's in many other countries; in France, for example. Shapiro's (1985) account of housing for the poor in Paris in the second half of the nineteenth century echoes many developments listed by historians of Britain: a rapidly growing urban population; the association of high rates of overcrowding and morbidity with poverty; initial attempts by government agencies to remove unhealthy houses while leaving their replacement to market forces; the movement to effective reform generated by fear of the poor as a threat to the established social order. It is perhaps the final feature which is more emphasized in the French situation, with a fear of the revolution constantly in the minds of the ruling classes. Government-inspired and philanthropic schemes to rehouse the poor met with less success than they did in Britain; home-ownership was seen as a powerful defence against socialism, but as in Britain, market forces provided no real solution against the killer diseases of cholera and tuberculosis, and it was not until the benefits of industrialization seeped down to the poorer segments of the working-class at the very end of the nineteenth century that real progress in health could be discerned.

In Eastern Europe the supply and allocation of housing has been based on very different principles from those prevailing generally in the West. A shortage of useful data has made evaluation of the Eastern European systems uncertain, but some key features do stand out:

1. housing has been available chiefly only to rent, and state agencies are major landlords, although unofficial sub-letting may be widely practised;
2. many cities contain housing markets where demand greatly outstrips supply, with the result that waiting lists are long;
3. flats are the commonest form of housing.

Very little market research type of data is available on how urban tenants feel about this.

The health consequences of this situation can only be guessed at, as can the changes resulting from the political upheavals in Eastern Europe at the end of the 1980s. It seems likely that when the Eastern Europeans, especially Russians, become more aware of the relatively affluent housing circumstances of the West, and are given increasing opportunities to improve their quality of housing and to alter the means of its distribution, powerful consumerist processes will be set in motion. Housing quality and distribution are quite likely to become subjects of much conflict and change in Eastern Europe between now and the end of the century.

The Third World is a different matter. Housing factors continue to make a major impact on health in poorer countries, with many similarities between Third World cities today and the British nineteenth century urban experience. Both involve rapid growth, in both the new arrivals have come predominantly from rural settings; and physical standards have left much to be desired.

The worldwide growth of cities has been a spectacular feature of late twentieth century life. At the beginning of the nineteenth century, the world's urban population was 50 million; today it has reached at least 1600 million, and is set to top 3000 million by the end of this century. By that time, 44% of the population of developing countries will be living in cities; Mexico City will contain 31 million, Sao Paulo 25 million, and 45 of the world's largest cities will be in the developing world.

City growth has come about in the Third World today, as in Britain in the nineteenth century, through the movement of people (many of them landless peasants) from the surrounding countryside. In Mexico City, where a thousand new arrivals turn up daily, they are termed 'parachutists' as they often appear at night suddenly in the squatter areas, as if they had fallen from the skies. Already over seven million people live in Mexico City in some form of uncontrolled or unauthorized settlement (Harpham *et al.*, 1988).

Many of the diseases of Victorian Britain have not been eradicated. Over 14 million children under the age of five died in 1986, many from conditions such as diarrhoea and measles which First World children easily survived (Hardoy, 1990, p. xix). A million cases of typhoid remain,

---

Housing design features and the diseases that they may help to overcome

Design features	Diseases combatted
Strong association	
Adequate supply of water	Trachoma, skin infections, gastroenteric diseases
Sanitary excreta disposal	gastroenteric infections, including intestinal parasites
Safe water supply	Typhoid, Cholera
Bathing and washing facilities	Schistosomiasis, trachoma, gastroenteric and skin diseases
Food production means	Malnutrition
Control of air pollution	Acute and chronic respiratory disease, respiratory malignancies

Fairly strong association

Ventilation of houses (in which there is smoke from indoor fires)	Acute and chronic respiratory diseases
Control of house dust	Asthma
Sitting of housing away from vector breeding areas (including stagnant water)	Malaria, Schistosomiasis, filariasis, trypanosomiasis
Control of open fires, protection of kerosene or bottled gas	Burns
Finished floors	Hookworms
Screening	Malaria

Some association

Control of use of thatch material	Chaga's disease
Rehabilitated housing	Psychological disorders
Control of heat inside the shelter	Heat stress
Adequated food storage	Malnutrition
Refuse collection	Chaga's disease, Leishmaniasis

Source: Stephens *et al.* (1985).

and in 1991 over half a million new cases of cholera (the vast majority in Latin America) were identified.

The new city dwellers bring little cash and few work skills with them. Illness rates among slum dwellers and squatters are often much higher

---

Housing in Addis Ababa, Ethiopia

Surveys of Addis Ababa, Ethiopia, in the 1970s found 79% of the population of one and a half million live in low-grade congested settlements of one-storey buildings under conditions unfit for human habitation. Houses are made of staves of wood covered with mud, straw and sometimes cow dung. The heavy rains sometimes wash away the mud plaster which needs continual maintenance. Often low-income areas can only be approached by rugged pathways which are inaccessible for service vehicles. Facilities such as sanitation, piped water and refuse collection are lacking. Of the population, 30% had no water supply, 24% had no toilet facilities, and only 35% of the solid waste generated in the city was collected and disposed of satisfactorily.

Source: Harpham, *et al.* (1988) pp. 30–1.

than those living in better-off areas. Harpham *et al.* (1988, pp. 47–50) give many examples. For many, housing conditions remain primitive.

Up to 60% of city dwellers may live in illegal settlements or cheap boarding houses. Many cities of over a million people may have no sewerage system at all. The cheapest housing is likely to be on unhealthy sites and inaccessible to emergency services. Vulnerability to periodic flooding or even earthquakes or volcanic eruption is not unknown. Many urban residents live close to environmental threats such as polluted water or noxious industries. Housing in these circumstances has a major impact on health.

Current concerns 2

2.1 UNFIT HOUSING

Legislating to condemn housing as unfit for human habitation, and destroying or improving it, has a history stretching back to the Nuisance Removal and Disease Prevention Act, 1855. Successive Acts have altered the definition of what constitutes unfit housing in detail. A subjective element has often been present, plus potential for disagreement between official and householder about what constitutes intolerable conditions for living.

While standards overall appear to have improved markedly in recent years, substantial pockets of unfit housing remain, and alarming claims concerning its effects continue to be made.

The box on p. 33 shows the current official definitions of what constitutes poor housing and Figure 2.1 presents the numbers of unsatisfactory houses, by various definitions, in 1986. Figure 2.2 shows the changes between 1971 and 1986. In that time the number of dwellings lacking amenities fell to just over half a million, only 19% of the 1971 level. Over the same period the number of unfit dwellings fell less dramatically to just over a million, less than 5% of the stock. Those in serious disrepair (also just over million dwellings) remained about the same.

In 1986 nearly two and a half million dwellings in England were assessed as being in poor condition: either unfit, or lacking in basic amenities, or in poor repair (defined as requiring urgent repairs to the fabric of the property estimated to cost more than £1000). Over 2 million had defects in their electrical system, and well over a million suffered from damp, inadequate heating, unsatisfactory stairs, steps or space, and insufficient facilities for waste disposal or food preparation. These defective houses were not distributed at random throughout the housing stock. Many were concentrated in inner city areas such Hackney, East London.

Some 14% of urban dwellings, but also 22% in rural areas, were judged

Definitions of poor condition properties

Properties which fall within one or more of the following categories:

Unfit	a dwelling not reasonably suitable for occupation because of problems with one or more of the following: disrepair; stability; dampness prejudicial to the occupier's health; internal arrangement; lighting, heating and ventilation; water supply; facilities for the preparation and cooking of food; sanitary conveniences and the disposal of waste water.
Lacking basic amenities	absence of one or more of the following: kitchen sink, bath or shower in a bathroom; wash hand basin; hot and cold water to each of these; indoor WC.
In poor repair	requires urgent repairs to the fabric costing more than £1000 (1986 prices). This definition of repair problems was introduced in the 1986 English House Condition Survey and replaced the 'serious disrepair' definition used previously. The two are not compatible.
In serious disrepair	requires more than £7,000 worth of work (1981 prices). This definition was used in the 1981 English House Condition Survey.

(Note: Definitions have changed for the two most recent English House Condition surveys, making comparisons over time difficult. The new fitness standard set out in the Local Government and Housing Act, 1989 redefines 'unfitness' to include houses lacking basic amenities.)

Source: Audit Commission (1991) Appendix 2, p. 37.

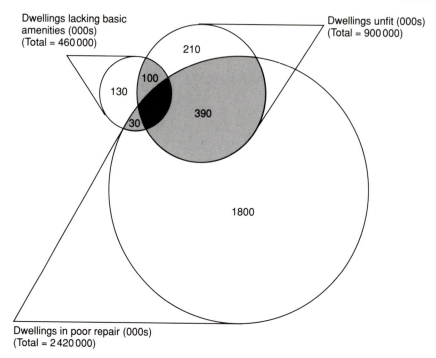

Dwellings lacking basic
amenities (000s)
(Total = 460 000)

Dwellings unfit (000s)
(Total = 900 000)

210

100

130

30

390

1800

Dwellings in poor repair (000s)
(Total = 2 420 000)

Figure 2.1 Numbers of defective houses in England, 1986. (From Audit Commission, 1991, p. 4.)

to be in poor condition. Occupants were more likely to be old, unemployed, or from ethnic minorities. Differences between tenancy categories were even more marked. Only 6.6% of housing association homes were included, and nearly twice that proportion (12.8%) of owner-occupied homes, which formed the absolute majority of defective homes. The greatest concentration of defective homes is however to be found in the privately rented sector. Harrison (1985) described conditions in Hackney.

Some 42% of privately rented homes were judged defective in the national 1986 survey. Dangerous conditions may be most common in houses which are in multiple occupation: large Victorian or Edwardian houses in inner city areas, for example, which have been converted into bedsits. A recent survey from the National Consumer Council, *Death-trap Housing* 1991, estimates some two million people in multiple occupation are in unsafe homes, at particular risk from fire. The Audit Commission (1991) suggest that as many as 180 000 houses (more than half of those in multiple occupation) may require attention. At the current rate of action it would take 15–20 years to bring about improvements in all of these, not allowing for others that will fall into bad condition in the meantime.

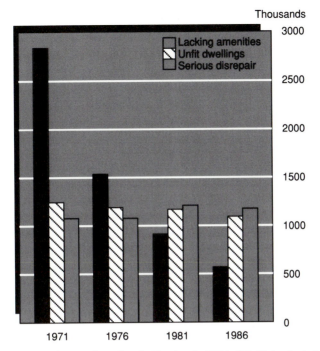

Thousands

Lacking amenities
Unfit dwellings
Serious disrepair

Figure 2.2 Unsatisfactory housing in England, 1971–86. Note that dwellings in poor condition can appear in more than one measure of unsatisfactory housing in any given year. (From English House Condition Surveys.)

Environmental health officers have a number of powers to deal with unfit or defective housing. Clearance programmes, popular in earlier decades to deal with whole areas of slum properties, are little used today. Even closure or demolition of individual houses, though possible to achieve, is seldom attempted. Under the Local Government and Housing Act, 1989, improvement grants can be made, targetted at houses in the worst condition and individuals in need of most assistance. Compulsory closure is usually adopted only when a landlord is unable or unwilling to bring his or her property up to standard, and even then the local authority may try to keep the property in use, perhaps by acquiring it and selling it on to a housing association for improvement and reletting (Audit Commission, 1991).

Little housing is, however, so unfit that it actually falls down, although the event remained not uncommon among Glasgow's tenement buildings until the early 1960s. Spectacular collapses since then have mainly been due to gas explosions rather than spontaneous structural failures. A notable example was in the high-rise block Ronan Point in East London, in 1968, whose significance will be discussed in section 2.5.

Hackney's housing remained, by national standards, appalling. In 1979–80 one in five dwellings in Hackney was unfit for human habitation – by far the highest of any London borough and more than twice the London average. Another 22% of dwellings were in substantial disrepair. In material terms that means sodden basements, leaking roofs, draughty windows, perpetually peeling paper and crumbling plaster: in human terms, damp, cold, rheumatism, respiratory diseases and depression. The National Housing and Dwelling Survey in 1978 found that more than 7% of households were overcrowded – occupied by more than one person per room. This was the third highest level in London, higher than any inner-city area outside London, and more than double the English average of 3.1%. Many of the families I met were sleeping three or more to a bedroom, several of them two or more children to a bed, a number of them sleeping and living in one room. Over 19% of Hackney households shared one or more than one amenity, lower than several traditional bed-sitter areas, but, again, higher than any district outside London and more than twice the average for England as a whole. In practical terms, this often means walking down one or more floors to toilet or bath, waiting around for other users to finish, and often, as responsibility for cleaning is confused, dirt and insanitation as well.

There are, too, other less commonly mentioned forms of housing deprivation. Most Hackney residents are denied the privacy and personal space which, in an era of increased egotism and reduced community solidarity, are essential to peace and sanity. Detached and semi-detached houses make up half the national housing stock: in Hackney they account for just over one-fiftieth. Only one in five dwellings, nationally, are flats, maisonettes or rented rooms. In Hackney, four out of five are, and in most cases they have no garden. In England as a whole, only 12% of households do not have their feet on terra firma, with the lowest floor of their dwelling at ground level. In Hackney, no less than 55% of household homes start on the first floor or higher, and 12% on or above the twelfth floor.

Two final statistics give some idea of the level of discontent. In 1987, one household in four was dissatisfied with its accommodation, the second highest figure in the country (behind Tower Hamlets by the tip of a nose). And the numbers on the borough's waiting list for council homes, 15 000 in 1981, were equivalent to the sum of all the households in private rented accommodation and all households living as part of another household.

Source: Harrison (1985) pp. 182–3.

The past and present state of private-sector housing is the key to Hackney's destiny. For, although council housing has now taken over the role of providing accommodation to the majority, it is through the private sector that new arrivals to Hackney gain access to council housing. It is the rooming-house that acts as the inner city's recruiting officer. This is the first filter that ensures that most newcomers will be among the poorest and most disadvantaged families in London.

The private sector, which comprises property built overwhelmingly before 1919, and most of it between 1860 and 1890, is in the worst physical condition. As we saw earlier, that is not simply a matter of age. A great deal of Hackney's Victorian housing was built on unsuitable ground, with poor or skimped materials, by cowboy builders of the day who did not care if what they built started to fall apart after a few years. A lot of the worst housing has done just that, a lot more was destroyed by the Blitz and more went under the bulldozer after the war. Indeed the present large extent of council housing in Hackney, as in other inner cities, is partly a product of the appalling state of the slums which it replaced. Nevertheless, there are still 24 000 private dwellings in Hackney and they house 63 000 people. Two-thirds of this stock, in 1980, was either unfit or in need of substantial repairs. Two out of five of its units were unfit for human habitation, and many of these would involve demolition or extensive rebuilding. One in ten was fit but lacked basic amenities. Another one in six required repairs costing £3000 or more. Within the private sector, it is the rented accommodation that is in the worst physical shape. In 1980 there about 5000 'houses in multiple occupation' (HMOs) in Hackney, containing more than one separate household. Almost half of these were the subject of enforcement orders from Hackney Council's environmental health department, requiring their landlords to remedy defects dangerous to life or health, to provide additional services, or to reduce overcrowding. In the Rectory Road Housing Action Area, only three out of 131 HMOs were considered to be in a satisfactory condition. In the Palatine Road Action Area, only 1 out of 92 required no action.In many others, the underlying troubles are concealed behind a dash of paint or a slap of rendering. The extent of the problem has led local housing associations to press for a special 'Hackney factor' to be added on to the normal government cost limits for rehabilitation work. Many of the brick walls are only 9 inches (23 cm) thick and, instead of being bonded together like most 9-inch walls, consist of two entirely separate skins, each $4\frac{1}{2}$ ins thick. The motive for this unorthodox method is to prevent the cheap and nasty second-hand bricks used for the inner skin from being seen on the outside. For the same reason, the front and rear elevations are often not bonded to internal walls or party walls, so they can move independently and bow out. Foundations are often inadequate, resulting in wall fractures, sloping floors, twisted roofs, back extensions pulling away from the main body of the house. Despite Hackney's high water table, damp-proof courses of any kind are virtually non-existent. The lowest metre of basement walls is frequently saturated and basement timbers rotted. Dry rot extends its cancerous white tentacles through many houses, digesting and cracking higher floors and ceilings. Roof slates suffer from 'nail sickness', a flaking around the nail.

In addition, the private rented sector also offers the most degraded human environment. In 1981, 6762 households (4% of the borough total) were occupying unfurnished rented accommodation. Overcrowding was not too serious (6%), But 23 had no bath, 12% had no inside toilet, 9% had neither bath nor toilet. The furnished rented sector was the most overcrowded in Hackney – 12% of the 5400 households were occupied by more than 1 person per room. Few lacked bath or toilet, but almost half had to share these facilities with other households.

Badly built in the first place, Hackney's Victorian terraces were badly maintained thereafter. Like clapped-out old cars, they were cheap to buy but very expensive to keep going in decent shape. Then, as the people who buy cheap houses, whether to live in or to rent out, are often short on income or capital, the essential maintenance simply was not done. Neglect was added to sloppy construction.

The end result is visible even to the untrained eye, in luxurious proliferations of lichens, moulds and mosses that would offer a fertile ground for botanical study, and abstract collages of crumbled, cracked and flaking paint, plaster, pointing and stonework.

Source: Harrison (1985) pp. 189–91.

2.2 HEALTH-THREATENING FEATURES OF HOUSING

2.2.1 DAMP AND COLD

The 1986 English House Condition Survey found that about 7% of homes are damp. A strong body of evidence, summarized by Smith (1989) and Lowry (1991), although not entirely consensual, documents the association of damp, cold and mouldy housing with poor health. Wheezing, breathlessness, cough, phlegm, meningococcal infection, respiratory

Figure 2.3 A wasted opportunity: flats which depend on the local economy to stay in use.

diseases, and a wide range of symptoms in children have been implicated. The association of damp and mould with childhood asthma has been repeatedly studied and this literature has been reviewed by Strachan (1991). However, recent research from Zimbabwe (Keeley *et al*, 1991) notes the virtual absence of childhood asthma in rural areas, and its association with urban wealth, not poverty.

Smith (1989) concludes that in Britain 'dampness is probably currently the housing factor with most far-reaching public health implication', although the causal mechanisms are often speculative and their plausibility remains to be established in natural science. Reporting bias may be involved; some of the studies rely on the subjective reporting of illness.

Hyndman (1990) reports on one such survey. She made a careful investigation of housing dampness and health among British Bengalis in Tower Hamlets, East London, surveying 345 people living in 60 flats, half of which were centrally heated. Damp housing was associated with subjective measures of ill-health. Hyndman also found an association between mould in the home and depression; hardly surprising, for as

Childhood asthma should be added to the list of so-called diseases of civilization, according to the authors of a study in 2000 primary school children in Zimbabwe. Keeley and colleagues found a 50-fold difference in prevalence of reversible airways obstruction (defined as peak expiratory flow below 2.5th centile for height before exercise, a rise of more than 15% after salbutamol inhalation, and a fall of 15% or more after exercise, with a subsequent rise after salbutamol) between children in a rural area (0.1%) and children in a rich urban area (5.8%). In children from a poor urban area the prevalence was 3.1%. In northern Harare, the only study area where there were white children, the prevalence was very similar between white (5.3%) and black children (5.9%). The authors attribute the differences to the far greater exposure of urban children to atmospheric pollution, such as car emissions, and to chemical additives in manufactured foods and drinks.

All the studies were carried out in a 3-week period at the end of the rainy season, when the prevalence of asthma was relatively high. Indicators of nutritional status were not significantly different between black and white children in the rich urban area of northern Harare but were lower in the (black) children of urban southern Harare and lower still in rural Wedza. Urban living and higher material standards of living, say Keeley *et al.*, appear to be associated with a higher prevalence of childhood asthma.

Source: D. J. Keeley *et al.* (1991) summary from *The Lancet* **338**, p. 1327.

Lowry (1991) has observed, 'The psychological consequences of having to scrape mould off the walls of your house every day are obvious'.

Much concern has centred on the fate of elderly people in winter. For every degree centigrade for which the winter is colder than average, there are about 8000 extra deaths. However, this excess winter mortality comes about through coronary and cerebral thrombosis and respiratory disease, rather than hypothermia.

Pointing out that the poorest 30% of households spend twice as much (as a proportion of their income) on heating than the remaining 70%, Lowry (1991) concludes that the people with least to spend (the unemployed, the chronic sick and the elderly) are also those who spend longest in their homes. While it is impossible to define a safe limit for house temperatures, risks of illness rise as the temperature falls. There would appear to be a strong case for ensuring that dwellings should be designed and equipped so that those inhabitants on the lowest level of income can maintain a minimum temperature of 16 °C/60 °F.

(a)

(b)

(c)

Figure 2.4 (a)–(c) Some effects of dampness in buildings.

2.2.2 INDOOR AIR POLLUTION

Some materials used in house construction (lead, asbestos, formaldehyde, for example) have been implicated in causing sickness. Attempts to make homes more airtight (e.g. by double glazing) to conserve heat and reduce fuel bills may increase health risks by releasing formaldehyde from cavity wall insulation or if asbestos is exposed following damage.

House dust mite antigen is known to be associated with asthma, and more commonly but less threateningly with allergies. A study of 68 asthmatic children found the presence of airborne antigen strongly associated with sensitivity to the mite; sensitivity to house dust occurred only at a lower threshold level than had previously been proposed as a risk factor, and even then not so strongly. Neither wall air humidity, central heating or double glazing had any significant effect on airborne antigen concentration. Price *et al.* (1990) suggest synthetic carpets may help the avoidance of antigens. Microbial contamination of indoor air can also cause legionnaires disease (a fuller discussion of legionnaires disease appears later in section 2.6.3) or humidifier fever. Living in a household with a smoker may endanger health, although demonstrating harmful effects experimentally can be very difficult. So also can putting across the message: only two thirds of Byrne *et al.*'s sample of Gateshead council tenants agreed that smoking can damage your health (1986, p. 85).

The threat from radon has been widely discussed. Radon is the single largest source of exposure to radiation for most people in Britain. It gets into homes from building materials and ground water, but the main source is soil gas. Its concentration shows great variation around Britain. The National Radiological Protection Board estimates that an annual 1500 deaths from lung cancer are caused by exposure to radon, but Lowry (1991) points out that there is no correlation between the distibution of mortality from lung cancer and exposure to radon. As with most other air pollutants, effects on health are so long-term that they are extremely difficult to measure with precision, and their influence may be swamped by other social and environmental pressures.

Gas cookers and paraffin heaters have been linked with respiratory problems, and occasional deaths are recorded, many of them in caravans or holiday homes.

2.2.3 FIRES AND ACCIDENTS

Some three million people a year have accidents at home which results in medical treatment, and about 100 people die each week as a result of domestic accidents. The cost is estimated at about £300 million a year in England and Wales alone. Children, old people and the poor are at particular risk, especially those in rented homes in multiple occupation. Some aspects of house design and furnishing are possibly significant threats to health: the use of glass in doors, window catches which small children can open, faulty electrical wiring, poor segregation of motor traffic from areas where children play, and the use of foam-filled furniture, now banned from sale in UK.

These hazards are likely to be present in temporary accommodation

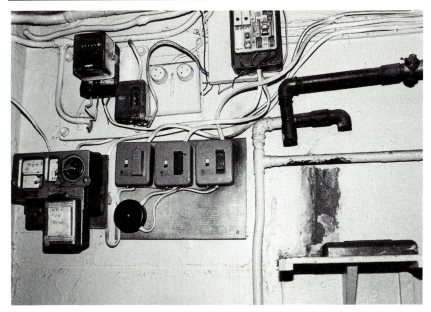

Figure 2.5 Failure to maintain gas and electrical supply lines effectively can threaten health.

(e.g. bed-and-breakfast hotels) into which homeless families may be directed. Such families may face additional hazards like makeshift cooking arrangements and unsafe electrical equipment. This situation will be discussed further in section 3.6.

2.2.4 INFESTATION BY PESTS

Proven cases where rats, cockroaches or similar pests cause disease are now rare in Britain, although press reports frequently suggest that such pests are becoming more numerous in British cities. Concerns over cockroaches have mounted as their presence has been reported from the Divis flats in Belfast (Lowry, 1991) and from Hackney in East London, where 30% of the tower blocks have been estimated to be infested. Cockroaches can move from flat to flat through cracks in the structure, or even through common flues; and the treatment of every flat in an infested block may be essential if they are to be eradicated. Obtaining entry to every flat can be a major headache for public health workers, and some tenants may feel the experience stigmatizing and resist entry. Council workers have had to resort to legal powers to gain entry; local authorities have found themselves, on the other hand, paying compensation to tenants whose flats have not been cleared.

Figure 2.6 Cockroaches are difficult to eliminate in tower blocks.

2.2.5 NOISE

Complaints to local authorities about noise have risen 20-fold in the last 20 years. Noise from neighbours is the commonest source, affecting 14% of adults in England. Noisy parties or barking dogs are frequent sources of trouble. One survey in London found 56% of those sampled had been annoyed by noise at home. Tension from noise can cause conflict between neighbours, and serious, even fatal, assaults have occurred.

Recent legislation has however, made noise a statutory nuisance, and local authorities are now obliged to investigate every reasonable complaint. Penalties for offenders can be very severe.

So far prosecution have been few. Remedial action appears to fall uncomfortably between the police and local authority environmental health officers, and the failure of authorities to provide a round-the-clock complaints service can make enforcement difficult (Godlee, 1992).

Physical problems stem from inadequate building materials, inefficient design, and poor construction standards, but human behaviour remains largely responsible, especially for the production of noise by electronic means. Modern appliances are powerful enough to produce a huge volume of sound, and some people appear to regard any restriction on their use as an infringement of their constitutional rights. Making very loud and continuous noise within one's own home may clearly restrict one's neighbour's rights to aural privacy.

2.2.6 PRIVACY

Summarizing the research on the desire for privacy, Allen and Crow (1989) conclude that privacy is a feature of domestic life to be greatly valued. This is especially true of young couples and their children, for whom living in an independent household is a strongly held ambition. Privacy involves being able to exclude the noise of others and controlling who enters the household's own space. An inability to control boundaries constitutes a threat to our self-worth; a feeling of personal violation is felt widely among those whose home has been burgled, for example. Privacy is a key element in the concept of 'home' (Rybczynski, 1988).

Less dramatically, restricting others' access may be desired to conceal failure to live up to expected standards of possessions, comfort or behaviour. One function of a garden, for example, is to provide a semi-public buffer zone to keep unwanted visitors at a distance. Fences and hedges are a defence. The unpopularity of open-plan estates is due in part to their failure to achieve this.

Privacy within the home for individual family members can be important too. Women may be especially disadvantaged, lacking any space of their own. Problems may become acute in communal living situations. However, too much privacy may be a bad thing; it may lead to feelings of isolation and loneliness. Home can become a cage or a prison as well as a haven. Both housewives and old people are in danger of finding their homes *too* important in their lives.

2.2.7 OVERCROWDING

As noted earlier, the Victorians feared overcrowding as a source both of medical and moral danger, permitting the transmission of disease and the moral corruption of the young.

Overcrowding is still seen as a threat to health, and is defined by statute and controlled by law. Living densities have been important in the spread of infection, most notably tuberculosis, even in the twentieth century. Recent research suggests a link with stomach cancer: in particular, among those whose homes in childhood lacked adequate food storage facilities (Barker *et al.*, 1990).

However, currently the threat is more often perceived as being towards mental health, although finding precise associations is a slippery business. Freedman, reviewing the literature in 1975, concluded that there was no evidence linking crowding with measures of stress or nervousness. However, human behaviour is complex, and problems associated with high density urban living (e.g. as indicated in the earlier section on noise) can be greatly ameliorated by material factors such as good soundproofing

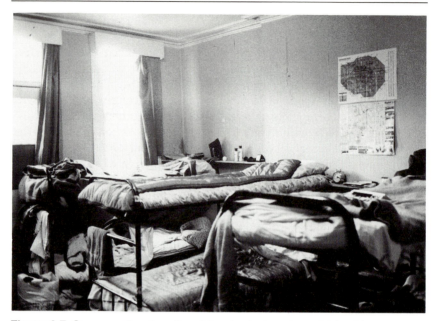

Figure 2.7 Overcrowding is a threat to physical and mental health.

between dwellings. With small crowded dwellings how they are used matters too. 'There seems almost a deliberate attempt to make each person's apartment a fortress; many inhabitants of high-rise, low-cost housing are like caged animals, making forays from their nests to get food or clothing, and then returning to safety', states Freedman (1975, p. 124). Gabe and Williams (1987) studied 452 women between 25 and 45 years of age in West London, finding a J-shaped relationship between crowding and General Health Questionnaire (GHQ) score. In other words, women who lived in households of less than one person per two rooms reported on average just under four psychological symptoms each; those living in rather more crowded households (up to one and a half persons per room) reported on average between two and three symptoms; and those in more crowded homes reported over six symptoms on average.

Just how stressful high density settlements are depends on a number of factors: the kind of population involved, the amount of time residents spend in and around their own home, standards of space and visual and aural insulation between homes, and design. Even at high density, people can suffer from isolation, but sensitive design should ameliorate this. Housing schemes should promote friendly contacts, where gossip and the development of acquaintances can flourish.

2.2.8 MENTAL HEALTH

The study of the geographical distribution of mental illness has a history of 50 years, beginning with the major enquiry in Chicago in 1939 by Faris and Dunham. Its findings, of the concentration of cases in poorer central areas, with rates decreasing towards the peripheral areas of the city, has been replicated many times. One distinctive confounding feature of British studies has been a concentration of cases in poor suburban council estates. The association of high rates of mental illness and low social class has been confirmed repeatedly by surveys, but the role of housing in this association is not easy to specify. Poverty is clearly a confounding variable. One of the most recent enquiries in this tradition, Birtchnell et al. (1988), found that among a large sample of young married women on a London housing estate that those who appeared distressed lived in poorer material circumstances. While determining the direction of causality of this association is not easy, it seems reasonable to assume that as the authors conclude: 'the accommodation itself played a part in the development and maintenance of the depression'.

Suburban housing estates have generated a long tradition of opposition on aesthetic grounds (Oliver et al., 1981). This has psychiatric parallels, deriving originally from Taylor's (1938) article in the Lancet, coining the concept 'suburban malaise', to be followed by its postwar cousin 'New Town Blues'. Freeman (1984) brings together some more recent critics: Mumford, who called the dormitory suburb 'an asylum for the preservation of illusion', the Marxists, offended by its emphasis on personal choice and private ownership, and a variety of sociological writers who see its cohesion based on fragile group pressures to conformity less preferable than a commitment to the vigour and heterogeneity of truly urban living.

Such a tradition has grown in peaceful times: during upheavals suburbs may develop new attractions because of their tranquillity and absence of danger. Civil unrest involving violence has been largely absent from British cities through most of the twentieth century. Northern Ireland is an exception, with communities divided on sectarian lines, and violence endemic over 30 years. The psychiatric consequences of this have been almost totally ignored. Among the few to take an interest have been Sluka (1989) and Blackman et al. (1989) who have described life in the Divis flats, an inner-city Catholic area of Belfast that has often been at the centre of violent events. Divis comprises one tower block and 13 seven-storey deck access blocks, 850 flats in all, home to over 2000 people. The constant threat and reality of violence, plus general poverty, has taken a considerable psychological toll. More than 70% of the households interviewed by Sluka had members who suffered from depression, bad nerves, insomnia, alcoholism, dependence on tranquillizers, or other psychological or emotional problems.

These symptoms arose out of a cocktail of problems which mixed psychological and physical stresses; poor construction and insulation against damp and cold, asbestos, sewerage problems, rats and cockroaches, poor maintenance, unemployment, poverty, frequent conflict with the heavy military presence in the area. Clearly babies born in the Divis flats have drawn the short straw in the lottery of British life.

Blackman *et al.* (1989) contrasted the health of Divis residents with those in Twinbrook, an almost equally poor estate in West Belfast which comprised houses with gardens. The Divis residents appeared to be in worse health according to both objective and subjective measures, and measures of health service use. Political and economic pressure led to the eventual decision of the Northern Ireland housing minister to demolish all the deck access blocks and rehouse their residents.

2.3 HEALTH INEQUALITIES IN HOUSING

Health inequalities in housing have a long tradition; their persistence into the 1930s has been documented earlier. The creation of the National Health Service in 1948 was seen by many as a way of bringing such inequalities to an end. Yet they have shown a surprising capacity to endure.

Most notably, the Black Report, commissioned by the outgoing Labour government in 1977, brought together evidence to show considerable inequalities in mortality and morbidity were widespread and enduring. The Report proved an embarrassment to the new Conservative government, which minimized publicity at the time of its publication and refused to endorse its recommendations. Subsequent publication by Penguin Books (Townsend and Davidson, 1982) ensured its wide circulation.

Inequalities in health were revealed not merely between different occupational classes but between the major types of housing tenure within each class. Thus, as shown in Table 2.1, men aged 18–64 have a greater likelihood of death if they are renting rather than owning their home, within each occupational class.

Tenure also appears to be a factor in the health of women. Evidence from the same study (OPCS's Longitudinal Study) found that women aged 15–59 were more likely to die if they lived in rented rather than owner-occupied homes. Table 2.2 gives the details. The findings apply when single women, working wives, and unemployed women are each considered separately.

Where other social differences are added, the health discrepancies become very wide indeed. Among single women and married women

Table 2.1 Standardized mortality ratio among males aged 18–64, 1970/75

Class	Tenure		
	Owner-occupied	Privately rented	Local-authority tenancy
I	79	93	99
II	74	104	99
IIIN	79	112	121
IIIM	83	99	104
IV	83	100	106
V	98	126	123

Source: OPCS statistics quoted by Townsend and Davidson (1982) p. 60.

Table 2.2 Standardized mortality ratios among women aged 15–59 at death, 1976/81

	Single women	Working wives	Jobless women
Owner-occupiers	85	79	84
Private renters	—	93	111
LA renting	129	99	130

Source: adapted from Moser et al. (1988) Table III.

without a job of their own, a combination of occupational class, housing tenure and car ownership resulted in differences of 250% in standardized mortality ratios. In other words, single women with a manual job and jobless married women whose husbands had a manual job, not possessing a car and renting their home, were two and a half times as likely to die before their sixtieth birthday as women in non-manual work (or married to such a husband), possessing a car and owning their home (Moser et al., 1988).

Payne (1991) considers that women's health is more influenced by tenure than men's: women spend longer in their home, and are at greater risk from their home's health-threatening features such as damp, noise and lack of somewhere for children to play. Women whose housing is poor have been shown to have higher rates of miscarriage, stillbirth, infant mortality and children born with congenital abnormalities.

Health differences in tenure carry through to early adult years. The National Child Development Study has been following the fortunes of 17 000 people born in one week of 1958. Recent research has compared the health of those who achieved owner-occupation, and those who have achieved a council tenancy, by the age of 23. By each of five measures – self-rating of health, hospitals admissions, height, the self-reporting of neurotic symptoms, and psychiatric morbidity – the health of the council tenants was poorer than that of the owner-occupiers, and differences were especially marked among the young women (Fogelman *et al.*, 1989).

Tenure can also be associated with health issues in the lives of elderly people. Many move on, when their health begins to fail, to sheltered housing schemes, which will be discussed in a later section. Others may wish to remain in the home they have bought, but find their finances increasingly stretched. Smith (1989, p. 51) describes recent developments.

> There is increasing interest in the use of home equity to finance long-term care. Further options for those whose health is progressively deteriorating, causing continuous or intermittent loss of earned income, might include the incorporation of homes within shared ownership schemes, and encouragement for local authorities to take equity stake in such properties, perhaps combined with a protected leaseback arrangement. These options might all help protect those whose health is already failing, from the stress and anxiety of losing their homes (as well as their pride and status) and from having to move away from existing networks of primary care and informal support.

Further inequalities occur within each housing tenure: some groups appear to contain a startling level of pathology. The cocktail of disadvantages faced by residents in the poorer parts of the council sector has already been touched on. In the study of the Divis flats in Belfast by Blackman *et al.* (1989) referred to earlier, no fewer than 16% of children had attended hospital in the month prior to interview, and 14% had been admitted.

Housing tenure is also associated with the prevalence of certain diseases. Cancer has been shown to be more common not only in lower social classes, but also among council tenants compared to owner-occupiers. The excess is to be found largely in smoking-related cancers. Owner-occupiers also survive most types of cancer for longer once it is diagnosed (Kogevinas, 1990).

Respiratory illness is also more common in council housing, as three studies – on difficult-to-let housing estates in Gateshead, a flatted estate in Liverpool, and a large sample from a number of towns – show. Children are especailly conspicuous sufferers (Smith, 1989, p. 22).

Entry into different tenures is made possible by very different routes. Owner-occupation has grown steadily: now it includes two-thirds of all households. It normally involves the ability to first raise a mortgage, and poor health may make this difficult; if for example, a manual worker cannot demonstrate his ability to earn high and consistent wages into the foreseeable future. It also leads to social polarization at a very early stage in the life-cycle, as has been well described: a young couple cohabit to economize on living expenses; after marriage they postpone childbearing, so that both can continue in full-time employment; relatively soon they can afford to buy a flat or a small house; over the years as mortgage repayments (reduced by tax relief) constitute a smaller proportion of income, their family expenses can rise and they may trade upwards to a larger house. Another couple with only slightly smaller resources or ambitions opt for tenancy, and are impelled towards the subsidized state sector because of the high costs of private rental housing; to qualify for the former they need children – so the wife ceases employment and family income falls; their chances of house purchase rapidly diminish unless they become eligible as tenants of long standing to buy their house at a nominal price (Amis and Lloyd, 1990, p. 291).

Health – or more precisely ill-health – is a most powerful factor in influencing entry into council tenancies. It has grown gradually in significance, most notably after 1945, but remains patchy in its scale.

The 1949 Housing Act allowed local authorities for the first time to cater for groups other than 'the working classes' but medical prioritizing gained momentum only with slum clearance programmes. The Chronic Sick and Disabled Persons Act, 1970 obliged local authorities to take account of disabled people's housing requirements, but gave little specific guidance as to how this was to be achieved. The 1985 Housing Act requires housing departments of local authorities to give 'reasonable preference' to certain disadvantaged groups, but provides guidance on the kind of priority in respect of only one of these groups, the homeless, who should receive priority if they are elderly, ill or disabled. Not surprisingly then, Smith, who provides a lengthy review (1989, pp. 34–47) of this topic concludes, there is little consensus on what constitutes 'vulnerability' and medical needs are viewed differently from authority to authority.

The potential dimensions of disagreement are many. Medical needs are viewed differently by different local authorities, which are themselves very varied in their allocation systems. Further, local authorities differ in the way they handle claims for medical priority. Some use date-order systems, some quota allocations for different groups, some have a points system. Among those with points systems, there is considerable diversity in the detailed working of the system. There is immense variety in the way health criteria are incorporated into the allocation procedure. There may be disagreements among the different types of medical workers – GPs, community physicians, health visitors – involved in making each local system work. Individual doctors themselves may be in conflict about the weighting and scale of medical factors in giving priority in allocation. Indeed it may be a manifestly impossible task to weigh the relative merits of different health problems and translate them into scores reflecting housing need.

Some commentators have suggested the game is not worth the candle: doctors should stay away from the business of assessing intending tenants.

Parsons (1987) lists the arguments against:

1. It may raise unduly the expectations of applicants;
2. It uses a lot of community medicine resources;
3. It may be used as a smokescreen to mask the effects of housing budget cuts;
4. There are no universally agreed procedures for carrying it out. Some authorities may make greater use of it than others. There may be special problems where local authorities and health authorities are not coterminous.

The other workers involved, local authority housing department staff, have equally few rules to guide their handling of cases and weigh health evidence. The involvement of environmental health officers has also been criticized as an inefficient use of their time (Audit Commission, 1991). It is hardly surprising if, given the scale of confusion and local variation, attempts to provide guidelines classifying claims have not been widely accepted.

Smith (1989, pp. 41–2) concludes:

> At every level, it seems that decisions concerning medical needs remain largely discretionary and somewhat arbitrary. Eligibility for priority status is therefore the outcome of a complex bargaining procedure between claimants . . . medical practitioners . . . and housing managers . . . In practice, allocations may be biased in favour of those among the medically deserving who are most skilled at mobilizing the medical priority system.

Despite all the confusion and uncertainties, surveys have found the proportion of applications seeking council housing who have included health reasons in support of their claim to have been considerable: between 13% and 70% (Smith, 1989, p. 36). Such figures may actually be underestimates of health problems among those seeking council housing (or rehousing). Among a group of council house tenants in Salford seeking rehousing, symptoms of mental ill health were found among 60 out of 64 applicants who had claimed medical priority, but also among 18 out of 26 controls who had not (Elton and Packer, 1987).

Yet, despite so much effort on the part of medical services, the proportion of tenants who are housed or rehoused on medical grounds appears to be only a small proportion of all of those who obtain council housing, although their waiting time may be shorter than other tenants (Smith, 1989, pp. 42–3).

The efficacy of rehousing in the improvement of health has been the subject of little good research, and what has been done suggests disappointing results, especially with respect to physical illness (Smith,

1989, pp. 44–5). People with neurosis do, however, appear to benefit (Elton and Packer, 1987). Given the large amount of medical manpower involved, providing other forms of health assistance may be more effective. Yet the dilemma for housing managers is even more acute and basic. Are they providing a service for social or medical casualties, or mass housing for the poorest quarter of the population? If they give undue preference to the first task, does it not weaken their ability to perform the second? Applicants whose only offence is an inability or unwillingness to achieve owner-occupation will feel unfairly penalized if they are constantly being driven to the back of the queue for their only alternative source of a good home, the council waiting list, by those who can plead grounds for special priority, such as sickness.

A further consideration is that those attempting to enter the council sector may suffer from a lack of knowledge of how the system works and how best to manipulate it to their own ends. Medical factors (in this case the absence of ill-health) may aid entry into another tenure, in this case owner-occupation. Buying a house usually involves raising a mortgage, and raising a mortgage usually involves evidence of high and consistent earnings at present and in the future.

The growth of owner-occupation has meant its spread down the occupational and financial scale. Yet fluctuations in property values and interest rates have resulted in more difficulties for marginal owner-occupiers and not surprisingly, the number of repossessions has in recent years (and starting from a very low base) risen sharply. In 1990 over 40 000 homes were repossessed, treble the previous year's figure. Current estimates are much higher. Many more owners remain in serious arrears. As Smith (1989, pp. 49–50) has pointed out, the breakdown in health of a crucial family member may play a part in many of these tragedies:

> For healthy owner-occupiers with a substantial mortgage commitment, the onset of chronic ill-health in any family member whose wage is required to sustain repayments, might bring seemingly buoyant housing careers to an abrupt end. At best, long-term illness might prevent expenditure on essential repairs, maintenance or improvements, or prompt a move downmarket; at worst, it could precipitate repossession and even homelessness. All these eventualities are, of course, just the kind of stressful life event now thought to exacerbate both physical disease and mental illness.

Official encouragement to local authorities to sell council houses to sitting tenants will have done little to reduce the differentials in health: indeed the result may have been an increase, as sales have been concentrated among the better quality council properties, and may have involved relatively healthy and wealthy tenants.

2.4 MOVING HOME

Dozens of surveys of moving house have been carried out, and reviews of this literature (Stokols and Shumaker, 1982; Heller, 1982; Smith, 1989) found, not surprisingly, that the health consequences are far from uniform, and seldom straightforward. Moving house can be exhilirating, especially for those leaving behind poor physical housing conditions, overcrowding, or neighbourhoods they have come to regard as unsatisfactory. It can also be a frightening step into the unknown. Leaving a loved home has been compared to a bereavement.

Much of the work describing the health consequences of moving house has concerned particular types of movement: that associated with the demise of slum or long established urban working class areas; movement into new suburban housing estates, either of owner-occupied or (more usually) publically provided rented housing; and movement into new satellite towns, again with a variety of occupancy types in different countries. Households moving into owner-occupation or the council sector may find they encounter particular difficulties, because of satisfying the criteria of access. Even becoming technically 'homeless' may be a fraught experience, which will be dealt with later.

The problem of elderly people who move home has been written about widely. Other groups, such as young single people, who may move out of their parent's house (or not) have received very little attention. Many studies report adverse consequences for health, especially mental health, and most especially if the move is enforced rather than entered into willingly.

An early example of the psychological cost of slum clearance is Thorpe's (1939) article, entitled 'Demolition Melancholia'. Thorpe investigated a number of cases of depression in Sheffield which appeared to result from compulsory uprooting from long established city areas to lonely new suburban estates. Elderly people particularly were unable to acquire the skills of making new friends and coping with the extra financial cost.

A larger-scale study of the psychiatric consequences of slum clearance was carried out among Italian-Americans in Boston by Fried (1963). Long-term grief reactions were noted among substantial numbers of this sample of over 500 people. Fried's work has been subjected to considerable criticism, notably by Key (1967), who considered Italian-Americans are both given to emotionality in verbal expression, and retain a recognizable sub-culture based on extended family and intense neighbourhood relationships. In fact they are the very opposite of the stereotypic isolated alienated or anomic resident of a slum area!

Key also makes methodological criticism of Fried's study: the language he used, e.g. 'How did you feel when you heard your house was to be torn down?' is unlikely to yield emotion-free responses.

Key's own sample of nearly a thousand families in Topeka who were forced to move house as a result of an urban renewal programme or road building reported a contradictory picture: their satisfaction with their houses increased after the move.

A third study of rehoused families moving out of a poor neighbourhood concerned a sample of 67 in Tel Aviv, Israel, who moved into more spacious apartments in a modern suburb. Like Key's, this study measured satisfaction with housing rather than levels of health. Findings were generally positive: families felt more satisfied with their new dwelling, and had invested in house improvements and new furniture. Satisfaction with their environment had however, declined. The authors (Yuchtman-Ya'ar et al., 1979) suggest this might have been improved if ex-slum dwellers had been scattered around the city rather than concentrated on one new estate, a solution which would have *increased* dissatisfaction amongst Fried's Italian-Americans in Boston.

Relatively little attention has been paid to how behaviour changes when housing circumstances alter. A perceptive account is given by a psychiatric social worker, Molly Harrington (1965) in her description of families moving out of decaying tenement blocks in Edinburgh into houses of a relatively modern and spacious kind. In the tenement home of two or three rooms, a mother might have to bring up a large family of five or six children. All available space is put to one essential use after another. The constraints of space affect the management of time. Arguments could be common over the use of facilities such as the kitchen sink, which served both for washing and the preparation of food. Personal activities which demand a degree of privacy, such as bathing of adolescent girls and sexual activities of parents, needed to be conducted with considerable discretion. In such circumstances, it was hardly surprising if out-of-home activities like drinking at the pub had a powerful appeal on husbands and fathers. Management of space and time are clearly important topics where homes are small and households are large. What might be seen as obsessional in one setting becomes a necessity in another.

Interest in the health of suburban estate residents goes back to work in the 1930s of M'Gonigle and Kirby, already quoted. Suburbs soon attracted attention for reasons other than the financial plight of residents called upon to spend more on rent and fares in their physically healthier new environments. These reasons centred around the loneliness, anomie and poor levels of stimulation that affected their residents, most notably the housewives for whom the new house could become something of a prison. Similar problems to those experienced by the sufferers of 'suburban neurosis' (Taylor, 1938) have been identified in post-1945 New Towns.

Careful scientific enquiry, however, while not revealing any particularly strong patterning of mental illness in suburbs, suggests it may be generally similar to patternings elsewhere. Taylor and Chave (1964) for instance, found that the prevalence of mild neurotic symptoms in an English New Town was similar to that found in most urban areas. Hare and Shaw (1965) compared the mental health of families in a new suburban estate in Croydon with that in an older decaying central area of the town, finding the two areas broadly similar.

Two studies of GP consulting rates report contradictory findings: a higher rate than expected, especially for mental illness, among 100 newly-arrived families in a Scottish New Town (Bain and Philip, 1975), but no increase in new illness among residents following their move to a sub-urban estate in Liverpool (Goodman and Crombie, 1982).

Two general points need to be made before concluding this section. Not all newly-arrived residents move in with the same expectations for the future, even in the most uniform surroundings. This is especially true of cheap owner-occupied estates whose population may be far from one-class: examples from the USA (Gans, 1967) and Australia (Richards, 1990) show different families arrive with different values, standards of behaviour and plans for the future. Even blandest suburbia's population is not as homogeneous as its housing.

Secondly, residents arriving at newly-completed estates of houses may find that the final details of building have not been accomplished, with a result that relationships with the developer or landlord are initially conflict-ridden. Hooper et al. (1978) describe an example, where com-munity organization became the residents' priority rather than help for individual families in settling in. Social work assistance may be hard to provide on such occasions if the social work authority is also the landlord.

Other studies have looked at the health of house-movers from particular perspectives. Probably the largest study ever carried out monitored changes in health among a sample of 400 black families in Baltimore who were rehoused into a new public housing project, and contrasted them with a larger sample who were not rehoused. Despite interviewing each family eleven times, and spending half a million dollars, the researchers were able to reveal only very modest differences in health (Wilner et al., 1962).

Finally a study already quoted (Elton and Packer, 1987) of applicants for rehousing in the council sector in Salford on the grounds of symptoms of non-psychotic mental illness found considerable improvement in mental health after rehousing. However, a control group who had requested rehousing without asking for medical priority also showed high levels of psychiatric symptoms, which reduced after rehousing.

Heller (1982) in a review including studies of people moving their job, patients discharged from long-stay hospitals, and people rehoused as a result of slum clearance, notes the poor levels of methodology in most studies. Both objective and subjective measures of success and failure are needed. Further longitudinal studies are required, a conclusion supported by others (Kantor, 1969; Hooper and Ineichen, 1979) who feel that too much research in this topic has been based to one-shot interview surveys. If Taylor and Chave (1964) for example had used a less blunt measure than 'under/over two years in residence' in their New Town Study, their findings might have been more precise and valuable.

The effect of moving long distances is particularly difficult to assess. International migration has a history as long as mankind's, and may be especially fraught when involving a move from countryside to city, or from living as a stable group following traditional lifestyles to being a member of a vulnerable minority in the midst of an alien culture.

Housing clearly has a role, but probably a minor one, in amongst such major changes. It may emerge more clearly as a subject of concern to migrants as they assimilate the norms of their host society and appreciate the relative deprivation of their new circumstances. On the other side of the garden fence, their host neighbours may denigrate the new arrivals for 'living in squalor', conveniently overlooking that their apparent poverty may be quite unasked-for; migrants seldom have any option but to start at the bottom of the pile.

One group whose mobility has attracted little attention is young people at the time they leave the parental home. Their very mobility makes them difficult to contact in large or representative samples. The housing circumstances of those who leave without telling their parents where they are going, the so-called 'teenage runaways' would be especially interesting to research. Their housing options are likely to be very limited, especially if their move has been from a rural or small-town setting into a big city. Their lack of resources may mean they drift rapidly into homelessness.

Another situation which has generated little curiosity among researchers is that of not moving, of staying put in stressful situations. Examples could be where eviction is a prospect, if financial resources dwindle (e.g. with unemployment or retirement) or if with illness or ageing and the decline of strength, the maintenance of an existing home becomes difficult, either physically or financially. Schemes have been created in recent years to help elderly people to remain in their owner-occupied home when living expenses exceed income. The creation of 'granny-flats' which permit an elderly relative to move into an annex of a family's home has been a solution for some households, both owner-occupiers and council tenants. However, what little research that has been done has shown that such arrangements are often plagued by practical difficulties (Tinker, 1991).

Figure 2.8 When everyone wants to move, no one can. How stressful is it?

2.5 THE HIGH-RISE EXPERIMENT

2.5.1 HOW DID IT HAPPEN?

During the last 30 years, advances in architectural technology, allied to changes in architectural fashion and distribution of political power, have changed the skyline of cities all over the world. Prefabricated techniques have made possible the construction of large numbers of high-rise blocks, for poor as well as rich, in cities in all five continents. Millions of people have had their lives significantly altered by these changes. In Glasgow, 263 blocks contain over 25 000 homes. In the London Borough of Newham alone, 111 tower blocks of 5 storeys or more have been built, housing almost one tenth of the entire population (Dunleavy, 1981).

During the last twenty years, a variety of studies from around the world have begun to present impressions of what the high-rise revolution means in terms of its effect on residents, concentrating on mental rather than physical health. Most studies have taken place in the UK, but others have been carried out in Germany, Canada, Israel and Hong Kong. What sort of psychiatric effects does high-rise living produce?

Before looking at each country in detail, the point must be made that those living in high-rise apartments are not necessarily typical of the wider population from which they are drawn. The British and Canadian studies all concern public sector housing, providing homes for a population which is essentially urban and poor. Some of the work in Germany has looked at the circumstances of British servicemen and their families stationed there. What people have moved from is also important. In some locations (e.g. Hong Kong, Israel) high-rise living has been imposed on populations with long traditions of high-density, multi-storey housing. Elsewhere high-rise tenants have moved from primarily rural locations.

2.5.2 THE EVIDENCE

High-rise living in Britain has been concentrated almost exclusively in the sector of the housing market provided by local authorities. Its development has been well described (Ash, 1980; Dunleavy, 1981). At its peak in 1966, the construction of 44 000 public sector high-rise dwellings was authorized.

Some of the high-rise's bad reputation in Britain stems from the methods of construction: poor quality concrete allowed water penetration, asbestos was used widely for insulation, difficulties were experienced with the heating. Other drawbacks are poor caretaking, poor rubbish collection, poor maintenance and fears over safety.

It is ironic than virtually none of the research into the harmful effects of tower block living was carried out in the early months and years of its development. Desire for high-rise living was never apparent among those destined to experience it. Surveys of housing preference dating back to Mass Observation's study in World War II reveal that for half a century British people have been stubbornly expressing their preference for a house with a garden, rather than a flat. For example, half of a sample of 64 households living in flats on overspill estates in Worsley, near Manchester, objected to living in flats. Most families with children thought flats were too noisy, too small, or not right for children. On the other hand, most single people and childless couples preferred flats as more convenient, easier to manage and cheaper to furnish (Cullingworth, 1960).

Subsequently, studies into high-rise and mental health have been carried out in London and half a dozen provincial cities. The Department of the Environment carried out a series of intellectually narrow but methodologically rigorous studies in the 1960s and 1970s on the effect of the built environment on behaviour. Some 1317 women and 369 husbands living on six new local authority estates in London and Sheffield were interviewed. Most lived above ground floor level. Almost half had suffered from a neurotic symptom in the past month, but incidence was not related to any particular building form, nor estate density, nor height off the ground (Reynolds and Nicholson, 1969; Department of Environment, 1972, 1975). A subsequent smaller project by UK government researchers (Littlewood and Tinker, 1981) found that families moving out of high-rise dwellings reported fewer symptoms of depression after the move.

Other studies were conducted by individuals or teams of academic researchers, in a variety of locations, using a variety of research techniques.

Bristol University researchers interviewed 262 women in 5 housing developments, in and around the city, and gathered written questionnaires from 234 husbands: 102 lived in a redeveloped inner city area; 40 in houses, 28 in low-rise maisonettes and 35 in high-flats. The remainder lived in houses on four suburban housing estates. Using a symptom check-list (similar to that used by the Department of the Environment researchers) the families in high-rise flats showed high levels of pathology, but those in houses in the inner city development showed even more. At reinterviews after three years in residence, many of the differences between sub-samples had been ironed out (Hooper and Ineichen, 1979) although large numbers of the high-rise families had moved out (Ineichen, 1973).

In Brighton, Bagley (1974) interviewed 69 women in a 12 storey block, contrasting them with 43 in houses. Flat dwellers were less satisfied with housing, environment and children's play space. They were also more neurotic, using the Eysenck Personality Inventory and GP consultation rates as measures.

Richman (1974) matched groups of 25 London families in high-rise flats, and houses. The high-rise group complained most about their homes, but it was the low-rise group which produced most mental illness in the mothers.

Gittus (1976) interviewed 344 mothers in Newcastle including 148 in high-rise flats. When comparing symptoms before and after the move, women and children in the high-rise flats were more likely to have an increase of symptoms than women and children in other dwelling types.

Hannay (1979, 1981, 1984) administered a psychiatric screening ques-tionnaire (the Foulds Symptom Sign Inventory) to a random sample of patients (964 adults and 380 children) registered at a health centre in Glasgow. Those living on higher floors (fifth or above) of high-rise flats had twice the prevalence of mental symptoms as those living on lower floors or in houses.

A study in Gateshead (McCarthy et al., 1985; Byrne et al., 1986) inter-viewed 383 families in 8 housing estates, including 174 in medium or high-rise. Overall, there was no relationship of symptoms with dwelling types: although flat dwellers reported more symptoms than house dwellers, differences were not significant and confined to some estates only. Finally, research in the high-rise Divis flats in Belfast revealed that many people, especially women, were suffering with their 'nerves'. While the physical environment appears as only one of a range of problems in their recent history, it is very probable that it represents an unsatisfactory solution to their housing needs following urban redevelopment (Sluka, 1989).

In Germany, Fanning (1967) and Moore (1974, 1975, 1976) studied samples of families of British servicemen stationed with the Royal Air Force. Fanning's research was among the first on high-rise living and mental illness to appear, and created a considerable impact, indicating both poor mental and physical health among families living on higher storeys. Moore criticized his methodology and produced findings of his own from the same location which were more ambivalent.

Williamson (1981) studied a sample of 430 high-rise residents (81% of whom were renters in areas in and around Cologne and Dusseldorf, and contrasted them with 166 controls. His paper is concerned more with factors in the sample which correlate with 'adjustment' rather than contrasting the health of the two samples, and his sample of relatively young, socially upwardly mobile residents appear happier in their high-rise location than most of the working class families interviewed by UK researchers.

Gillis (1977) studied a large sample of Canadian public housing tenants, all parents with children living at home, finding an association (for women but not for men) of height in the block with signs of psychological distress.

Mitchell (1971) interviewed large samples of flat dwellers in Hong Kong. Emotional health appeared to be adversely affected in multi-storey buildings, although in part this might have been due to overcrowding, especially when families had to share a home. There is wide agreement that family cohesion helps people in Hong Kong to tolerate high-rise high-density living, but little attempt to back the statement with sound research. Chiu (1988) studied 260 suicide attempts in 1986 but found that fewer of them lived in public housing blocks, compared with the rate from the general population. Neither was there evidence that would-be suicides lived on higher floors.

Churchman and Ginsberg (1984) surveyed 344 middle class women in high-rise blocks in Israel; 92% were owner occupiers. While no data specifically on mental health is presented, their informants, like Williamson's Germans, give a strong impression of a much more favourable perception of the environment in and around their home than are conveyed by the great majority of working-class samples reported from elsewhere.

2.5.3 LESSONS LEARNED

Some research has shown an association between poor mental health and living in high-rise apartments; some has shown no association, and there is no evidence of negative association. The general conclusion to be drawn from this literature is that high-rise living appears to have an adverse effect on mental health, in some circumstances. However, quantifying this adverse factor is extremely difficult, and the following considerations must not be ignored.

1. Constructing sound research projects in this area is difficult. Most high-rise living is provided for the urban poor, whose health in relation to other sectors of the population is likely to be worse. The inverse association of social class and mental health has been well-documented from all over the world; in the UK, even with a 40-year history of free health provision, major differences between social classes in physical health remain (Townsend and Davidson, 1982). Public housing is often allocated on the basis of need, so that tenants may be in poor health when they move in. It is important to distinguish between the effects of *moving* home (discussed in the previous section) from the effects of living in a *particular* home. Moving into high-rise homes has been observed to produce an increase in symptoms (Gittus, 1976) and moving out a decrease (Littlewood and Tinker, 1981). Sutton (1988) found no significant difference in GP consultation rates after moving out of high-rise flats for a Newham sample.

2. Despite the range of studies quoted, the experience of high-rise living among many groups remains relatively unexplored. The poor geographical spread of research is unfortunate and the absence of research from the USA and USSR especially so. Most studies have concentrated on the experiences of young families, especially mothers. Perception of their children's satisfaction with their environment may be a key factor in determining the satisfaction of adults (Ineichen and Hooper, 1974; Birtchnell *et al.*, 1988). Behind the well documented low level of satisfaction with high-rise living among families with young children (Jephcott, 1971; Gittus, 1976; Bromley, 1979; Marmot, 1983) is the awareness that the circumstances for the mothers of young children in high-rise flats are uniquely isolating: the weakness of the solitary nuclear unit of father, mother, and young dependent children in Western society has become a sociological cliché, and the mother's isolated domestic experience in a high-rise is its extreme manifestation.

   Although the quality of much of the research is variable not all studies show a pattern of poor adjustment (Williamson, 1981; Van Vliet, 1983). Translating concepts such as adjustment into specific measures of health may not always be feasible.

   Childless and single-person households have been scarcely explored. Very little work has been done with middle-class families other than the German and Israeli work quoted.

Figure 2.9 The triumph of the motor car. No defence, no garden, nowhere for children to play.

3. Design features of high-rise housing are clearly important. The basic need for each family to preserve its own living space is shown by the Hong Kong research (Mitchell, 1971). Preserving privacy by adequate sound-proofing is another self evident need. Efficient and controllable areas around the home are widely recognized as important. Basic provisions (safety for children, reliable lifts) are recognized by all, including middle class families (Churchman and Ginsberg, 1984). Other features concern what residents and visitors do. Jephcott (1971) points out the need for places 'that lend themselves to a bit of gossiping'. Many blocks are so rigid in design that no attempts at do-it-yourself improvements are possible. And the idea of 'defensible space' (Yancey, 1971; Newman, 1973) where residents can monitor and if necessary regulate who comes into the block has become influential in their design and refurbishment. Buildings providing for few households (irrespective of density) may encourage both greater sociability and a greater sense of responsibility among residents (Freedman, 1975). Coleman (1985) in an exhaustive study over 4000 blocks, found both size of the block and a series of design features

Figure 2.10 Defence at a cost of dullness and uniformity.

affected the scale of overt social malaise exhibited by graffiti, vandalism and the like.

4. The construction of high-rise developments has often meant the break-up of long established urban working-class communities and the decline of rural villages. In many cases the first residents of high-rise blocks came to live, perhaps for the first time in their lives, among strangers. This exacerbates feelings of alienation and loss of control (Freeman, 1984, p. 38). As we saw earlier newly arrived tenants may be poorly equipped to deal with problems calling for corporate action (Hooper *et al.*, 1978).

5. High-rise blocks and problem estates are not synonymous. Poverty may be a greater demoralizing force than the design of the housing environment (Morris and Winn, 1990).

The full political history of the high-rise revolution remains to be written. We have little detail of its influence on population movements. In the Third World it may be associated with providing additional resources for the poor moving off the land into cities. In industrialized countries, high-rise blocks have often been provided to replace old single-family

Figure 2.11 Adding an external lobby increases a house's defence.

housing. Yet what little research on consumer choice that has been done has suggested that this was not what residents wanted. No formal machinery for recording the views of tenants and intending tenants existed, with government departments relying on the often unsubstantiated views of 'experts' on what user needs were (Marmot, 1983). At the height of the high-rise boom, decisions to go ahead to build were steam-rollered through and objections brushed aside.

As Freeman (1984, pp. 215–6) has expressed it:

> Local authority housing managers knew well enough that flats were unpopular as homes for families, but they were ignored as being men of little faith. . . . Occupants who protested were told that they were 'selfish' or 'behind the times'. . . . Whole communities were swept aside to make way for large new structures which were with few exceptions, tasteless, shoddy and totally without character.

In Britain early objections such as those against high density by Glasgow's Medical Officer of Health in the mid-1950s were brushed aside (Dunleavy, 1981). Delay in publishing some research in the early period of construction may have been crucial in pushing through the entire

Figure 2.12 An improved entrance, but designed in, rather than tacked on, would have been better.

programme (Ash, 1980). The partial destruction of Ronan Point in East London in 1968, causing the deaths of 5 residents and injuries to a further 17, hastened a change of opinion away from high-rise, and subsequent discoveries of major faults in many blocks led to a rapid conclusion of the building programme.

Some high-rise blocks, Ronan Point and its neighbours among them, have been destroyed prematurely as residents could not be found for them. The same process has been taking place in USA, where the award-winning scheme of Pruitt-Igoe in St Louis is among the more famous. Some became so unpopular that the actual act of destruction was presented as a lottery prize.

As Freedman (1975, p. 120) has pointed out, failures tend to be more publicized than successes. Decline can sometimes be reversed. Sutherland (1986) has described the effect of introducing entryphones and better security measures in high-rise blocks in the Gorbals, Glasgow. Morale improved although as Sutherland concludes, better technology alone is not sufficient. Such modest upgrading exercises have subsequently been carried out in many places.

Another example from France provides ground for optimism. The

---

Refurbishing tower blocks

In January 1989 a middle-aged couple in a high-rise block in Stockwell, south London, died when petrol was poured through their letterbox and set alight. Firemen could not rescue them as they had barricaded themselves in behind a steel grille, because they feared a break-in. A neighbour was later jailed for their manslaughter, and the two teenagers he had paid to pour the petrol received four and a half years in youth custody.

The tragedy prompted a visit from a Home Office minister, and a campaign by residents to improve their conditions, resulting in a £3 million refurbishment scheme involving electronic surveillance systems (operated by the tenants' TV sets), reinforced doors for each maisonette, new entry hall, and a concierge. Break-ins, previously running at the rate of two a week, are now rare, and the morale of residents has improved greatly.

Source: Jenkins (1991).

---

development of La Democratie, just outside Lyon, provided homes for families moving into the city from the countryside, and for migrants moving to France from abroad. Unemployment, racial tension and delinquency were rife during the 1970s, and by the early 1980s many of the flats were empty. However, following the planned destruction of 4 of the 14 blocks in 1983, and a series of environmental improvements and community projects, the drift away of population was halted and the crime rate cut (Webster, 1983), although unrest has subsequently flared up again.

It seems reasonable to assume that levels of mental illness in such circumstances would have been altered more by changes in the social and physical environments of people's homes rather than their height off the ground.

2.6 HOUSING AND THE ENVIRONMENT

Where you live, as well as the kind of home you live in, may affect your health. The surroundings of a person's home are a great influence in deciding how dissatisfied or stressed many people are in living where they do. They have been shown to be especially important for the residents of high density, redeveloped inner city areas (Department of the Environment, 1972; Coleman, 1985). A survey of the 383 council tenants in Gateshead found their satisfaction with their home was determined more by its location than its type or the presence of structural defects. People living in 'difficult-to-let' housing areas reported more illnesses

(a)

Figure 2.13 Design stresses and satisfactions. (a) Handy open spaces; but whose? (The sign reads: 'The use of this green for exercising dogs is prohibited and legal proceedings will be taken against persons whose animals are found to foul this amenity area'.)

and inferior health status than did people living in other housing areas. Consistent differences between housing areas could be explained more by the location of a dwelling than by its type (Byrne *et al.*, 1986).

Very few people remain totally oblivious to where they live. Feeling will be generalized so that sorting out precisely what people like about their area, as what particularly troubles them about it, may not be easy to specify. However, some particular environmental features have been identified as affecting health adversely.

2.6.1 NOISE AROUND THE HOUSE

Noise problems between immediate neighbours have been discussed briefly in section 2.2.5. Noise from traffic or street repairs can also be stressful. In 1990 the deputy mayoress of a northern town was

(b) Priorities for parking and pedestrians may be unclear

fined for threatening to castrate a gas board worker with a kitchen knife after building work had been going on outside her home for four months. Regulation of noise in and around the house, in contrast to at the workplace, has received little attention from measures and legislators.

2.6.2 ELECTRICAL SUPPLY EQUIPMENT

This has emerged recently as a possible threat to health, apparently enhancing the risk of certain physical and mental diseases, although little can be said about the causality. One literature review (Coleman and Beral, 1988) found electrical workers appear to show a slightly heightened risk of leukemia, especially acute myeloid leukemia. There appears to be no increased cancer risk for people living near electric transmitters, except perhaps for those living very close. A study of residents in tower blocks in Wolverhampton (Perry and Pearl, 1988) found an excess of cases of depression and some types of heart disease among those living close to the main electricity supply cable. All agree that the literature on this subject is conflicting and confused.

(c) Living on a busy road: problems with parking and crossing the road safely

2.6.3 LEGIONNAIRE'S DISEASE

Legionnaire's disease is named after its identification following a meeting of the American Legion in 1976. Some cases at least can be clearly identified. Legionnaire's disease can be acquired by inhaling infected droplets of water, although the precise transmission route is often unclear. Outbreaks occur from time to time, with the source of infection often remaining undiscovered. Other cases occur on a sporadic basis.

Domestic sources of infection are usually identified as hot water systems. Other environmental sources outside the home may also be implicated. Bhopal *et al.* (1991) made a careful study of 107 cases in Glasgow, taken out of a sequence of 210 between 1978 and 1986, discounting cases that arose during major outbreaks or were acquired abroad, or whose diagnostic criteria could not be agreed. They found a clustering of cases in the proximity of cooling towers: 500 metres seemed the crucial danger range. They discount explanations based on such populations being more susceptible to infection, as there are apparently few cases on suburban council estates; or of cases coming to light as a

(d) Open space, a long view, but probably high property values

result of more rigorous testing. They suggest that better maintenance of such towers is needed.

2.6.4 POLLUTION FROM NOXIOUS INDUSTRIES

This was a very common general threat in the nineteenth century. Many public health measures have come about as a result of studies of workers in various dangerous industries (Wohl, 1983). Risks have grown in the twentieth century, especially around nuclear-powered installations.

The greatest disaster has been Chernobyl (1986) in the former USSR. In Britain fears have centred on the nuclear processing plant at Windscale, now renamed Sellafield. Most recent research suggests that children of male workers at the plant have been suffering from an increased risk of leukemia.

The most spectacular non-nuclear disasters of industry in recent times have been at Seveso, Italy in 1976, when dioxin was sprayed into the environment from a broken safety valve at a chemical factory. Many animals died, including 80 000 chickens. The factory owners paid out $25 million in compensation to nearly 6000 claimants for sickness and damage.

The disaster at Bhopal, India in 1984 was even worse. Following a leak of lethal chemicals from a storage tank, over 2500 people died, thousands more were affected, and many continue to suffer long-term (Hazarika, 1987).

Small-scale industrial pollution remains an everyday threat but its presence is so taken for granted that it excites little public interest. An escape of poisonous gas from a chemical factory in Liverpool in December 1991, for instance, resulted in 11 people going to hospital, but earned no more than a passing mention in the national press.

2.6.5 POLLUTED RIVERS

Rivers have been used as dumping grounds, effectively industrial sewers, since the growth of large-scale industry (Wohl, 1983, Chapter 9).

A spectacular disaster occurred at Camelford, Cornwall, in 1988 when a lorry driver accidentally discharged 20 tons of aluminium sulphate into the water supply, turning the water for 20 000 people into a mild sulphuric acid solution. Half the population suffered immediate symptoms; some found their hair turned green. Years later, dozens are still suffering from signs of minor brain damage, and many more from tiredness and arthritis. Controversy still surrounds the extent to which the 1988 disaster remains responsible for the enduring problems.

Living on the margins 3

Several vulnerable groups can be identified in urban-industrial society as having special housing needs, and requiring specialized help in housing. Most numerous of these groups are the frail elderly. Rather more recently the mentally ill, the mentally handicapped, the physically disabled, and the terminally ill (notably AIDS sufferers) have been identified as other special groups. The policy of closing large institutions for a number of these dependent groups has transferred many people out of hospital into alternative forms of 'community care'. In reality this puts many of them into rundown 'ghetto' areas of cities. Housing options (e.g. hostels) that are available are likely to be heavily concentrated in the decaying cores of large cities (Dear and Wolch, 1987). Living a genuinely independent life on meagre resouces may in such circumstances be simply impossible.

3.1 THE FRAIL ELDERLY

For a number of reasons some elderly people have become identified as a group needing specialized housing help. People are living longer and the number of elderly people in British society has been growing quickly as a proportion of the population. Secondly, the health of elderly people, although improving, is not as secure as that of younger people. More of them are incapable of living without the active support of healthier (usually meaning younger) people. The rise of the medical specialisms of geriatrics and psychogeriatrics have indicated the response of the medical profession to this new demand on their skills. Thirdly, the fragmentation of family life through the shrinking of household size means that an increasing proportion of old people are either living alone or living with a frail and elderly partner. Often their housing is of poor standard: the English House Condition Survey 1986 found that one in five pensioners living alone lived in houses needing at least £1000 to be spent on them.

Homes whose fabric, fittings and furnishings are poorly maintained are likely to produce additional health risks to the people who live in them. Falls are especially common among old people, and adaptations of their environment (especially for those with poor eyesight or restricted mobility) and alarm systems for those living alone can be extremely valuable in preserving their quality of life.

Some trends indicate improvements in the housing circumstances of elderly people: increasing home ownership, earlier retirement, higher pensions and greater affluence for many. For about 10% of elderly people, especially the middle class, retirement is a time of change of address, and the form this takes for many is retiring to the seaside. Such migrations have a long history. Defoe noted in his 'Tour through the Whole Island of Great Britain' in 1724–6 that areas on the eastern edge of London such as Stratford were expanding rapidly as rich citizens from the capital built large second homes there 'for the pleasure and health of the latter part of their days,' (1971, p. 48). Some seaside areas are now so heavily settled with elderly people that a considerable additional burden is placed upon Social Service Departments, for example in Sussex's 'Costa Geriatrica', where over a third of the population are of pensionable age. Many moves are made in relatively young old age, immediately on retirement, without much thought for the dislocation of relationships that is likely to follow, and without considering the effect of subsequent deterioration in health.

Groups of old people have always been segregated by their housing. Whereas some of the wealthy have moved into hotels, the poor were forced into the workhouses. Nowadays a range of segregated options are available: nearly 10% of over 75s, and over 20% of over 85s were in institutions of one sort or another at the 1981 census. Altogether some 5% of pensioners are in institutional care, and as many again are in sheltered housing.

Sheltered housing is the least supported kind of residence for those unable to cope in their own home. Often a dozen or more dwellings are provided on the same estate (many are purpose built) and one dwelling is occupied by a warden who keeps a daily check on the old people. Some schemes are provided by local authorities, but in the 1980s increasingly by housing trusts or charities. Schemes appear generally popular, and many have long waiting lists. Applications have tended to come from increasingly sick and disabled elderly people, increasing the workload of wardens (Farquhar, 1990), although one recent study (Macdonald et al., 1991) found that among a sample of 276 residents and their partners in sheltered housing in Scotland, 29% had a zero level of dependency, and another 27% a low level. Among the residents of 200 'amenity' dwellings (specialized housing for the elderly possessing similar standards for space, heating and aids, but lacking wardens, alarm systems or communal facilities) 60% had a zero level of dependency and 21% a low level. Macdonald *et al.* (1991) speculate that this apparent low level of dependency may result from the premature deaths of more dependent partners, leaving healthy survivors in residence, or that the high proportion of relatively fit tenants in both kinds of schemes may reflect admission policies that have been designed deliberately to keep the warden's task in bounds.

More supportive environments are provided in residential or nursing homes, where skilled staff (qualified nurses in the latter case) are provided around the clock. Some are state institutions, provided and managed by local authorities (residential homes) and the NHS (nursing homes). Some are run by charitable or religious organizations, and some (a sharply increasing proportion) are commercial enterprises. They are housed in a wide range of buildings, ranging from converted workhouses which go back to the nineteenth century to modern purpose-built establishments. Residents are generally of a level of frailty appropriate to the care provided, but this is not always the case: there is considerable overlap. Dementia is common in virtually all settings. Surveys of local authority homes record up to 70% of residents suffering from some degree of cognitive decline (Ineichen, 1990). Increasingly institutions of all kinds for the dependent elderly have to provide for the failing mental powers of residents. Specialist institutions for the care of the demented are to be found in both state and private sectors.

3.2 THE MENTALLY ILL

Special housing provision for mentally ill people suffering from conditions other than dementia have existed for many years, but the scale of provision has increased dramatically since the number of people in psychiatric hospitals peaked in the mid-1950s.

Most of the research which has covered this process has been very restricted in its scope, so that attempting to answer a question such as 'How successful has it been in providing the kind of housing needed by discharged hospital patients?' is not easy to answer. Some studies of long-stay groups discharged into carefully prepared settings (e.g. Jones, 1985; Gibbons and Butler, 1987) appear reasonably successful. Others indicate some cause for concern.

An example of the letter is the study by Hatch and Nissel (1989) of 215 short-stay patients discharged into Westminster in the latter half of 1988. They found housing the most conspicuous gap in provision. A quarter of the sample were homeless at admission and this proportion did not fall on discharge. The supply of supported accommodation only catered for those thought to need it. Until more comprehensive accounts of community housing projects begin to appear, the question of how successful they are at meeting the housing needs of this group of people remains largely unanswered. The simple fact remains that not enough housing appears to be available for this vulnerable group.

The questions of whether or not the adequacy of community care was fully validated and the extent of persisting demand for hospital care among those with chronic or incapacitating psychiatric conditions, remain open to discussion (Dear and Wolch, 1987). Many mentally ill people figure among the homeless; this will be discussed further in section 3.7.

3.3 MENTALLY HANDICAPPED PEOPLE

A policy of reducing the numbers of the mentally handicapped, or people with learning disabilities, living in hospitals, with the aim of the ultimate closure of the hospitals, has been pursued by successive British governments since the late 1960s. Numbers in hospital have fallen from 59 000 in 1969 to an estimated 27 700 in 1989.

Most of the discharged residents, and many younger people with learning disabilities who cannot, or do not want, to live with their relatives, need homes with staff who will continue to look after them. Some schemes provide round-the-clock care, others provide help at certain times of the day only.

The speed of change of service provision has varied over space and time. Four fifths of the schemes for independent living in Kirklees (Huddersfield and Dewsbury) have come into being since 1983. They are varied in type: villas attached to hospitals and social service hostels are not all alike, they differ widely from one another, and cannot be assumed to be less institutional than hospitals. However, they represent, collectively and individually, opportunities for people with learning disabilities to live a life as far as possible untrammelled by the rigid rules of residential institutions, and to enjoy as much independence and autonomy as is practically feasible (Booth et al., 1990).

Many different agencies – health authorities, the local authority Social Service and Housing Departments, housing associations, charitable bodies such as MENCAP, commercial firms and private individuals – may all find a niche to contribute to the variety of home situations that are needed. As well as arranging an appropriate placement for each person, those responsible for setting up such services will need to recruit well-motivated staff, choose residents so that friendships will flourish, and monitor progress so that independent living brings with it personal development, and greater feelings of self-worth for people who may have been understimulated and devalued in hospital.

3.4 THE PHYSICALLY DISABLED

The number of wheelchair users has risen from 1.2 per 1000 (1960) to 4.0 (1970) and 7.2 (1986). There are 400 000 in Britain of whom 60 000 are totally reliant on wheelchairs. However, not all physically handicapped people are wheelchair users. They have a variety of needs and make use of a range of services.

Morris (1991) reports on a survey of the needs of 55 disabled adults in Camden who were the clients of various services. Half lived alone (or with a personal assistant) and 60% were in council property.

The sample show a high level of disability. All need help with repairing, decorating and maintaining their homes: nearly all need help with housework, three quarters with bathing, and half with going to the toilet.

Over half reported that adaptation had been made to their home, but most of these claimed further adaptations were required. Altogether 37 (67%) wanted adaptations to be made: mostly changes to the bathroom, access to services such as electricity or refuse collection, and door openers or entry phones. Most felt adaptations would not be forthcoming as the necessary grants were unobtainable. Many faced difficulties over getting out from their home to a vehicle.

Only 9 (16%) wanted to move home, generally to somewhere entirely on ground-floor level. However nearly half (42%) felt they might have to move in the future.

Clearly disabled people are entitled to every assistance to let them remain in their desired homes if this is practicable. 'Ghettos for the handicapped' must not be created.

3.5 THE TERMINALLY ILL

Neither home nor hospital are always suitable or available for the terminally ill. The response has been the creation of the hospice movement, and more recently the provision of specialized housing situations for AIDS sufferers.

Smith (1990) points out that people with HIV have claims to be treated as having special needs but also face discrimination in mainstream housing markets. Young people have low priority for council housing, and HIV acts as a barrier to obtaining a mortgage. A variety of organizations are working to produce a variety of housing options for AIDS sufferers, reflecting the heterogeneity of their needs (Smith, 1989).

3.6 THE BUREAUCRATICALLY HOMELESS

This category refers to those who have registered with, and been accepted by local authority housing departments as homeless. Acceptance as homeless means that the local authority will assume the obligation to house such people, but initially in many cases this means living in cheap hotel accommodation where normal domestic life is virtually impossible.

The numbers of those accepted as homeless by local authorities has been rising steadily. In 1989, local authorities accepted as homeless and found accommodation for 148 000 households, more than twice the number in 1980. Of these 134 000 were priority need category, 11 000 more than in 1988. Of those families in priority need, 80% either had or were expecting children: more of the remainder included households which were vulnerable because of old age, physical handicaps or mental illness, or were homeless in an emergency. Homeless families were awarded over a quarter of council properties becoming vacant, against 16% in 1981/2. Over a half had become homeless as relatives or friends could no longer accommodate them, and another quarter because of the breakdown of a relationship.

As well as the 148 000 who were rehoused, 65 000 were given advice and assistance, and another 71 000 applicants were deemed not to be homeless.

At the end of 1989, 40 000 homeless households were in temporary accommodation, compared to about 4500 in 1980. Of these 12 000 were in bed-and-breakfast accommodation and another 9000 in hostels; 62% of households in temporary accommodation were in London. Local authorities were paying out £137 million a year for keeping homeless families in bed-and-breakfast accommodation.

Reasons behind the steady rise in homelessness include a steady decline in the number of houses to rent, as the private sector of the market has contracted, and a million local authority council houses have been sold off. The rented share of the stock has shrunk to 33%. Other factors include the breakup of families, increasing poverty, the closure of large psychiatric hospitals, and the rising mortgage interest rate, which has had a severe effect on the poorest families sucked into owner-occupation in the housing price boom of 1987–8. At the time of writing, repossessions are continuing to increase in numbers, with no end in sight.

Homeless families are not found uniformly scattered around the country. They are concentrated in the cities, and within the cities in poorer areas. For many the solution has been in the short-term to place them in hotels which provide a bed-and-breakfast service only.

This is clearly unsatisfactory for a number of reasons. First, it is expensive for local authorities, far exceeding the cost of housing these families in conventional flats or houses. The difficulty in maintaining surveillance over such arrangements is difficult, and provides easy opportunities for fraud. Secondly, such environments are quite unsuitable for the happy upbringing of small children, or indeed for any kind of family life on a long-term basis. Rooms are cramped, cooking and washing facilities minimal. There may be considerable restrictions placed on the movement of families; for example, they may not be allowed to stay in during certain times of the day. Thirdly, such hotels may be some distance from the family's home areas. Of the 600 hotels used in London, 200 are in the Paddington and North Kensington district (Victor *et al.*, 1989). This may make it difficult not only for displaced families to keep up their normal contacts with relations, but for health and welfare services to be delivered effectively. Paddington and North Kensington District is one of the poorest in the country and serves a most varied population: mothers of over 70 different nationalities give birth at the local hospital, St Margarets (Hibbitt, 1990). Fourthly, the temporary nature of the arrangement adds a cost to the stability of the family's organization, especially at a time (when children are very young and babies are being born) when this is most essential. Bed-and-breakfast living is not always temporary, of course: it may go on for several years.

A study convened jointly by the London Food Commission, Maternity Alliance and Shelter (Conway, 1988) permits a graphic description of what homelessness means in practice for family life and health.

A sample of 57 homeless families living in 38 bed-and-breakfast hotels were interviewed; 22 were from ethnic minorities; 34 of the households were headed by couples, and 23 by lone women. Altogether there were 71 children, and some women were pregnant.

All the families were, by comparison with the rest of the society around them, very poor. Only nine had a member in work, and all the jobs were poorly-paid ones. The physical conditions were grim: most shared a bathroom and toilet with other households, a significant number with at least ten other people. Cooking facilities were poor, preparing food was difficult, and six households could not make even a hot drink. Nearly half the households were beyond the legal limit for overcrowding. The report's verdict is that conditions could 'only be described as appalling'. Families therefore faced problems of poor diet (four out of five felt they were eating less well than before), fear of fire or other accidents, little domestic security and a lack of control over their living space: noise and lack of privacy on one hand, and for some families a ban on inviting visitors into their home on the other. While such problems may have been bearable in the short-term, the families had no way of knowing how long they would need to endure these conditions. Some had been living where they were for two years. Costs to health were obvious: headaches and migraines, diarrhoea, chest infections, feelings of irritability, tiredness and exhaustion were common. Health problems in pregnancy were difficult to treat. One in three were unhappy with their access to medical care. GPs and health visitors shared the families' concerns.

The effects on health have been summarized: homeless women are twice as likely to have problems and three times as likely to need admission to hospital during pregnancy as other women. A quarter of babies born to mothers living in bed-and-breakfast accommodation are of low birthweight, compared with a national average of less than 1 in 10. The children are more likely to miss out on their immunization, while poor sanitation and overcrowding encourages the spread of infectious and diarrhoeal illnesses. Good nutrition is almost impossible because of poor facilities for storing and cooking food. Accidents are common among the children, and parents often suffer from depression (Lowry, 1991). A recent study from St Mary's Paddington (Paterson and Roderick, 1990) found that although homeless pregnant women suffered from considerable disadvantages (late booking, more previous obstetric problems, more low birthweight and premature babies) they did not appear to experience significantly worse obstetric outcomes.

Various obstacles make obtaining primary health care difficult for homeless families. Some are told that the arrangements are temporary, so they may not even try to get registered with a GP. Many who do try give up after a few rebuffs from doctors unwilling to take such 'problem familes' and few realize that the local family practitioner committee will find them a doctor (Lowry, 1991).

Some families may be registered with their new GP only on a temporary basis, which means their records are not transferred.

A number of local responses have been described. In Bayswater, West London the Family Practitioner Committee has drawn up a list of local GPs who will accept homeless patients. The Bayswater Hotel Homeless Project pays GPs for sessions at a special surgery. When a family attends it is temporarily registered with a doctor on duty, and after three months permanent registration is arranged.

Other responses include the appointment of a salaried GP in Finsbury Park to service homeless families and advance their interests among other health workers; and the introduction of regular surgeries at a large hotel for the homeless in Hounslow. Summing up new developments in healthcare for the homeless, Smith (1989, p. 63) concludes 'These *ad hoc* solutions seem to work but they are inherently fragile', and that what is needed, short of an end to the system of housing the homeless in temporary locations, is a mechanism to force GPs to grant equal rights of access on their list to homeless patients, and a reduction of the spatial concentration of homeless people in particular areas.

Difficulties are particularly acute in providing preventive or screening services. Hibbitt (1990) describes how ante-natal care was supplied on a drop-in basis, which had only limited success. She lists a sample of the extremely practical needs which mothers themselves identified.

1. A washing line to hang across the window or room for drying clothes and stergene for washing as the hot water invariably ran out.
2. Two dustbins with large plastic liners: one for household rubbish and waste food, the other for dirty nappies.
3. To learn how to bathe the baby in the sink or washing-up bowl.

4. The necessity of having two sterilizing tanks as anything that fell on the filthy carpet (often having been sprayed with insecticide against an army of cockroaches, etc.) should be sterilized.
5. How to get the baby used to the constant noise and glare it was subjected to from radio, TV and overhead lighting.
6. How to gain access to other services and to learn if they even exist.
7. What to do about registering the father's name on the birth certificate without threatening DSS benefits.
8. How to cope with feelings of isolation, depression and frustration.

Acceptable standards of primary health care for homeless families need a readiness to help for all the workers involved, and good communication between them. Patient-held records may also help. But the new GP contract, giving incentives to GPs to achieve high levels of preventive health measures, will not encourage them to admit patients perceived as problematic (such as homeless families) on to their lists.

Finally, even hospital care can sometimes present administrative difficulties. The under-use by homeless families of primary health care services means that hospital services may be relatively over-used; but out-patient referrals are often not taken up, and where out-patient waiting lists are long, those with no fixed address may have moved on before they can receive notification of their appointment (Smith, 1989). Proving eligibility for treatment may be difficult if hospitals practice a severe policy of only treating residents of a specific catchment area. But in a study of Paddington and North Kensington, homeless patients occupied almost a tenth of all hospital beds, and were high users of casualty and paediatric clinics (Victor *et al.*, 1989)

The situation may actually be even worse than it appears. Connelly *et al.* (1990) show that statistical returns from housing authorities may be inaccurate, and the use of households as the basic unit of homelessness makes estimating the number of persons involved, impossible. Details like age, sex, social class and ethnic identity are nowhere provided.

The poor level of statistical information generated by housing authorities about homelessness is made worse by staffing problems in Homeless Persons Units. Health authorities have, as a result, little ability to provide either unbroken medical care for homeless families, or the knowledge needed either to plan services or deploy resources most effectively.

A recent development has been the shifting by housing authorities of homeless care from bed-and-breakfast hotels to private leased accommodation. This will both benefit homeless families, and lower the authorities' cost, as rent for leased property can be recovered from central government via housing benefit. However at the time of writing central government was taking steps to restrict this action.

3.7 PEOPLE LIVING ON THE STREETS

No one knows how many people sleep on the streets in Britain every night. The 1991 Census found 1275 in London alone, but previous estimates have varied. Once on the streets it is hard to keep healthy. The shelter, warmth and privacy often taken for granted do not exist; good food may be hard to find or expensive; it is almost impossible to keep clean; minor illnesses are hard to cure (Lowry, 1991).

Documenting the precise levels of health of those sleeping rough by conducting reliable health surveys is even more difficult than doing the same for homeless families living in bed-and-breakfast accommodation.

A succinct literature review is provided by Doggett (1989). Between a third and a half of people living rough are thought to have serious health problems, and as many as one in 20 have at least four health problems at the same time.

These problems are extremely varied, but tuberculosis and other respiratory problems are both very common and very persistent. Among vagrants and hostel dwellers numerous studies have shown high rates, with up to a 50 times increased risk.

Another common problem of those sleeping rough concerns their shins, legs and feet. Of one sample, 21% had severe foot problems. Another is gastrointestinal disorders with 11% of one sample suffering from peptic ulcer (Toon et al., 1987).

Frequent accidents are one reason why homeless people often have to be referred to hospitals. One in seven of Toon et al.'s sample were referred to hospitals, where for a variety of reasons, many did not receive appropriate treatment.

Street dwellers may suffer from a greater excess of mental than physical illness, which may have been exaggerated by the pressure to reduce the numbers of patients staying in psychiatric hospitals. Distinguishing cause and effect is not easy. The prospect of sleeping on the streets, friendless and penniless for even a few nights, would be construed as a threat to their mental health by many adults.

It is therefore not surprising that few attempts have been made to assess the mental health of street dwellers in Britain, although American studies have shown rates of up to 40% estimated to be mentally disabled (Dear and Wolch, 1987). An opportunity to test a British sample was taken recently when hundreds of homeless people came together for the annual Crisis at Christmas event. Over a third of those examined were psychotic, a fifth had positive symptoms of schizophrenia; and a quarter had severe physical problems, yet two thirds of them had had no contact with medical services. Even some of the psychotics had never been in contact with the services. Many of the older homeless have lost all contact with their own relatives, friends and sources of social support; many of the younger have grown up in care. Over 90% came from outside London. There are several times as many men as women (Weller *et al.*, 1987; Weller, 1989).

Among related problems alcoholism is extremely common and drug abuse particularly difficult to treat (Doggett, 1989 pp. 348–9). Other problems which affect health are of course present among those sleeping rough. The Centrepoints survey in 1990 found that among those using a young people's shelter, two-thirds had no home to return to; 41% had grown up in care. Recent changes in social security benefit will make assistance more difficult for some to claim. The civil authorities may be not merely uncaring but positively hostile. In 1990, 1426 young people were prosecuted for begging and sleeping rough. Drifting into prostitution remains a possibility for young people of both sexes. No agency of public assistance seems prepared to grasp this particular nettle: both public and political attitudes suggest indifference.

Homelessness is extremely common in many cities of the developing world: an estimated 100 million adults and 80 million children. The births and deaths of many may not be recorded, so the problem is under-estimated. Malnourishment may project health problems into the next generation.

3.8 RESIDENTS IN HOSTELS FOR THE DESTITUTE

Little recent evidence is available on the physical health of this group. Shanks (1988) provided a GP service to 6 hostels and 2 day centres in Manchester between 1979 and 1982. The annual consultation rate was 3.4, significantly higher than expected compared to the general population, but significantly lower after controlling for social class. Class-adjusted figures for each disease group show an excess of consultations for communicable, haematological, psychiatric, genitourinary and dermotalogical diseases, and a statistically significant lower rate for other disease groups.

The strengths of this study include the long time-period under consideration (two and a half years) and the diagnosis being done entirely by one doctor. Providing regular care (twice weekly surgeries in the two largest hostels and once weekly elsewhere) is shown to produce quite high levels of consultation as his service became well-known and accepted. Secondly, the distribution of types of disease appears very different in this group of patients from that of the general population. Individual consultation took longer than with other patients often due to lack of communication, bizarre behaviour, and drunkeness, coupled with the need for detailed explanations and personal counselling.

Rather more interest has been shown in the mental health of hostel dwellers: surveys have been conducted by Marshall (1989) in Oxford,

Timms and Fry (1989) in Waterloo, London, and Teeson and Buhrich (1990) in Sydney, Australia.

Marshall studied 48 medium- to long-term residents of two hostels selected out of a total of 146 on the basis of their persistent severe mental disability, and difficulty in coping independently in the community: 22 had entered the hostels via the local psychiatric service, and another 7 had travelled the same route via other local services. Only five had never been psychiatric in-patients. A history of drug or alcoholic problems was common. Within a 2 week period, 23 were recorded as talking to themselves; 20 displayed verbal aggression, and 12 were sexually offensive. Overall, their behaviour and skills resembled those of long-term psychiatric patients. Marshall pointed out that 'the two hostels, staffed by psychiatrically untrained workers and volunteers, were effectively attempting to do the work equivalent to that in two long stay psychiatric wards, while also caring for another 98 homeless residents, many of whom have considerable problems with substance abuse. A follow-up study 18 months later (Marshall and Gath, 1992) found that most had remained in the hostel, without significant differences overall is their level of behaviour. Only 10 had been rehoused. Although one in three showed a poor outcome of marked deterioration in behaviour, a long stay in hospital, or death.

Timms and Fry (1989) carried out a briefer survey in a Salvation Army hostel in Waterloo, central London, in 1986–7. Large numbers appeared to be mentally ill, with schizophrenia an especially common diagnosis (see Table 3.1).

Table 3.1 Mental illness among residents in a Salvation Army hostel

	N=	Schizophrenia (%)	Other psychiatric diagnosis (%)	No psychiatric diagnosis (%)
New arrivals	65	25	38	37
Established residents	58	37	10	53

Source: Timms and Fry (1989), p. 70.

The authors suggest that such institutions may be able to cope with such a high level of psychiatric morbidity, because they exhibit two features which are strikingly reminiscent of the old mental hospitals: the wide range of bizarre behaviour tolerated, and the general non-intrusiveness of other residents and staff.

These aspects of hostel life might well result in an emotional climate, similar to those where low expressed emotions can reduce the likelihood of relapse and which can be subjectively comfortable for the schizophrenic. However, the lack of appropriate stimulation means that no progress is made towards rehabilitation or resocialization.

Teeson and Buhrich (1990) administered the Diagnostic Interview Schedule to a sample of residents in the largest and cheapest shelter for homeless men in inner city Sydney. They found 21% earning a diagnosis of schizophrenia and another 5% probables. This is both an increase on the findings of a similar study in 1983, which found 14% plus 2% probable; and in the author's view an underestimate of the true prevalence, as one third of those sampled failed to complete the interview. Altogether only 64 out of the 116 men called to interview completed the DIS.

Teeson and Buhrich do not consider that the increasing numbers of mentally ill residents at the refuge are due to the programme of deinstitutionalization, as only three of their confirmed schizophrenics had had a prolonged psychiatric admission. Rather they blame pressure on cheap rented accommodation in Sydney, which has made it both dearer and harder to obtain. The poor quality of residents' social environments may make it more difficult for them to leave.

Providing health services for hostel dwellers has been the subject of considerable recent enquiry.

GP registration has often been noted to be low, but a recent programme of encouragement in Bristol has shown a heartening increase in registration, in an area where more than one in ten of the population live in temporary accommodation. Vassilas and Cook (1990) attribute this success to the encouragement by hostel staff for residents to register with a GP; and the ready availability of members of the inner city mental health team, who can be reached quickly in either the local health centre or a local hostel.

At a drop-in day centre in Soho, Central London, it is the familiarity of staff which appears to win favour with its clientele, mostly single men from the North of England, Scotland and Ireland, who despite obvious mental health problems may not wish formal referral to a psychiatrist (Joseph et al., 1990).

Williams and Allen (1989) evaluated two schemes in London where a multi-disciplinary primary health team was provided directly to homeless people through day centres, night shelters and hostels. The service was in general appreciated by its clients who felt it did not stigmatize them, and fitted in well with their lifestyle. The views of other health workers were more mixed. And of course the service did not reach homeless people who did not visit the locations where it was offered.

Williams and Allen conclude that some sort of outreach service is needed but its does not follow that a special team, separate from mainstream services is the best option. A greater emphasis on nursing and psychiatric care appears to be needed.

Women hostel dwellers are fewer in number than men, and their needs may have been relatively neglected. James (1991) reviews the literature on the subject and describes his attempt to provide a regular psychiatric service to the residents of a hostel in south-east London. He found mental illness common, and in the opinion of the hostel staff, becoming commoner in recent years. Although the staff were dedicated, and exceeded their contractual obligations, the facilities at the hostel were clearly inadequate for the psychiatric needs of the residents. James concluded that for this group of women, psychiatrists should be more assertive; much psychiatric pathology remains untreated, and psychiatrists should seek out their patients, rather than the other way round.

Recent responses from the Department of Health to the problem of the mentally ill homeless have included the funding of a series of specialist hotels; the establishment of multi-disciplinary psychiatric teams, plus an evaluation team, in inner London; and the development of the 'Care Programme Approach' which puts the responsibility for achieving appropriate accommodation for patients accepted by specialist psychiatric services in the hands of a key worker (Kingdon, 1991).

3.9 TRAVELLERS AND OTHERS

There may be more than 12 000 travelling gypsy families in England and Wales. Providing health care for them can be particularly difficult. Local authorities are obliged to provide sites, but not all do this, and many authorized sites lack basic amenities. Many authorities are prepared to evict families even with babies or pregnant women, from unauthorized sites. There are obvious difficulties in getting medical care to people who are permanently mobile. Harrassment is a further problem some travellers have to face (Durward, 1990).

As with other marginal groups, travellers are difficult subjects to research thoroughly. One attempt in Kent in 1984 interviewed 263 mothers (Pahl and Vaile, 1988). Over half felt there were practical and environmental problems in looking after their children, and some lived in 'horrifyingly poor' environmental conditions. A substantial minority (between 1 in 7 and 1 in 3) lacked running water, electricity, toilet facilities or rubbish collection. While 85% were registered with a GP, perinatal and infant deaths, and low birthweight babies, were much commoner than national figures, and immunization and breastfeeding rarer.

A wide review of the literature on traveller health (Feder, 1989) compares the unsavoury campsites to shanty towns in the developing world. Poor child health, large families, general poverty, widespread smoking, local opposition to travellers, and difficulties in achieving health care are also noted.

Other groups on the verge of homelessness include residents of women's refuges and squatters. Many residents of shanty towns in Third World cities may also have only a tenuous hold on their right to live where they do. In all but a technical sense, these groups might be said to be homeless.

The difficulties of conducting valid health surveys in such settings are obvious: investigations of mental health rather than physical health are extremely rare. Reichenheim and Harpham (1991) are a notable exception: they administered the Self-Response Questionnaire (a list of 20 questions dealing mostly with psycho-emotional disturbances and calling for a 'yes/ no' answer) to a sample of 480 mothers of children under 5 in Rocinha, the largest squatter settlement in Rio de Janeiro, Brazil. Because of the low level of the subjects' literacy, the test was actually administered by health workers.

Some 36% of the mothers were rated 'probably mentally ill' for scoring at least 8 positive (i.e. ill) answers. This is a high rate compared to other community studies. Probable cases were found more often among the poorest mothers, and those living in bad environmental conditions.

Conclusions 4

What are the influences of housing upon health? Certain themes stand out: the influence of housing on physical health; the influence of housing on mental and emotional health; health-related design features of housing; the association of housing and poverty; housing for disadvantaged groups; blurring distinctions between owners and renters; growing public awareness of health issues in housing; and the changing role of public health agencies.

4.1 THE INFLUENCE OF HOUSING ON PHYSICAL HEALTH

Clearly the kind of circumstances that prevailed in nineteenth century British cities, and in many Third World cities today, show how massive this influence can be.

Housing affects health most seriously when physical conditions are bad. The population is most vulnerable when population densities are at their highest, and when urban growth is at its fastest. High population density, rapid population growth, and a young and poor population structure make a potent cocktail; mix them all together and the prospects for health are explosive.

When such conditions are present, the universal needs for housing to answer – adequate shelter and interior space, warmth, privacy, running water and sanitation, plus less essentially electric power and adequate transport – must be provided for. Not providing them can mean disease on epidemic scales. In Britain today the most serious environmental threats to health associated with housing have passed, but the current health situation in many cities of the world today has many similarities to that of early Victorian Britain, but magnified a thousand times over:

> Three quarters of the cities that contain more than five million people are in developing countries. In these cities there are an estimated 100

million homeless adults and perhaps as many as 80 million homeless and in many cases abandoned children. 25% of the people in these cities have no safe water and 40% lack access to sanitation. About 30% of the solid waste lies uncovered in the streets. Children brought up in these circumstances have 40 times the mortality of other children. In many cities in the developing world air pollution is a much graver problem than it is in Western cities. Prostitution of both sexes and by no means excluding children is rife. (Acheson, 1990, pp. 1484–5)

But Acheson is not totally pessimistic despite the fact that the world's population is increasing at a quarter of a million a day. He feels that expansion will level off in other countries, as it did in Britain early in the twentieth century. Others are less sanguine.

Hardoy *et al.* (1990), for instance, forecast that hundreds of millions more people will be living in urban squatter camps. Cities will be not allocated sufficient power from central governments, to ensure that environmental developments are regulated to protect health; local authorities' power will be especially weak around the periphery of cities, where urban population growth will be most intense. City funding will be insufficient to provide adequate healthy housing and prevent the growth of unregulated homes, so that communities will grow without the means to provide a decent infrastructure. Unlike nineteenth century European towns, they are not supported by buoyant economies. Even if the state, or commercial builders, could provide adequate housing for urban workers, few of the new townsmen would be able to afford the rent. Even in times of affluence economic growth cannot ensure that housing conditions for the poor will improve. In Seoul, South Korea, housing conditions actually deteriorated at a time when the economy was experiencing an unprecedented boom (Hardoy *et al.*, 1990).

Some needs – fresh water and sanitation – are universal. By and large these have been met in Britain, and in many other industrialized countries. Problems of damp housing, occupied by tenants who cannot afford to remedy them, remain. Some other aspects of the physical quality of housing, such as the danger of fire, or the threat of infestation, also need improving. Other major problem areas concern more subjective needs, such as adequate space and warmth, which are more difficult to measure. Appropriate standards may in part be culturally determined; perceived need will grow as affluence grows.

4.2 THE INFLUENCE OF HOUSING ON MENTAL AND EMOTIONAL HEALTH

Looking after mental and emotional health is important too, and rises in significance as physical needs are met. Studies quoted earlier have shown how mental illnesses are not distributed equally throughout the population. Living alone, living in overcrowded accommodation, and living in council housing are all related to higher psychiatric prevalence rates (Thornicroft, 1991).

Environmental factors are implicated in the basic causality of certain mental and physical illnesses, and affect the course of many more. One social and environmental feature that affects illness and morale is a sense of belonging, a feeling of being part of a community. This need comes strongly to the fore as more tangible needs are taken care of.

Langenback (1984) points out that the perceptions of environments among people who live or work in them may not correspond to those of the powerful groups possessing the ability to change them radically. Industrial landscapes in the North of England, long considered by many to be ugly and dirty, evoke fond memories among their residents. What the planners saw as suitable locations for comprehensive redevelopment, as sites of undesirable exploitation of the workers, the workers themselves might regard with warmth and nostalgia. The meanings attached to buildings can be symbolic as well as realistic. It is noteworthy that clear signs of a lack of concern with the environment around homes such as the presence of litter or graffiti are common in many modern high-density developments but very rare in areas of individual houses (Coleman, 1985).

Expressing a sense of community is not an easy matter. Precision is almost impossible. To what group should people feel they belong – their street; their neighbourhood city nation; even continent? Answers may differ among individuals. Some people may feel the need much more strongly than others.

The growing size of cities, the continuing fluidity of national boundaries, and enduring controversies over ethnic groupings can all confuse the application of simple labels in people's search for identity. In many parts of the world, even nationality is far from secure. Whole groups (often very poor to begin with) may be forcibly uprooted. Some examples in the contemporary world such as the Palestinians are well-known. Others, like the several million refugees from civil war and failed harvests throughout Africa, receive much less publicity, except when extreme famine affects a small proportion of them. The Kurdish community in Iraq is the latest group to lose their homes. Recent political developments in Eastern Europe suggest that the large-scale uprooting of populations in Yugoslavia may be repeated many times over in the not-too-distant future.

Belonging also has its dark side: who gets excluded? White (1986) describes his fiercely patriotic 'poor but loyal' supporters of the British Empire in Campbell Bunk between the wars as antagonistic to Irish, Jewish and black people to the point of violence. Exclusions from certain life-style options, such as living in particular house-types or locations, is

Figure 4.1 Victorian terraced housing: sense of community – or rows over parking?

likely to affect the health of those excluded adversely, especially if they feel their rights are being unjustly restricted, although gathering evidence in support of such a statement is not easy.

4.3 HEALTH-RELATED HOUSING DESIGN

Housing design has traditionally been associated with health through an insistence by official agencies on achieving rising standards of space, and an obligation put upon builders to increase basic amenities, in matters of sanitation, water supplies, gas or electric power, and light. Very little attention has been paid to the idea of comfort: a historian of the concept of 'home' (Rybczynski, 1988) remembers it being mentioned only once in a six-year architectural education. Yet 'comfort' (a concept embracing convenience, efficiency, domesticity, physical ease, privacy and intimacy) is for him the core concept in the notion of home.

Comfort has proved easy to find in the suburban semi-detached housing which has remained extremely popular in Britain for some 70 years. Many of the post-World War II developments provided by the council

Figure 4.2 Space and variety; desired qualities of urban living.

sector have been much less successful, and this is a verdict which is not limited to high-rise flats.

One aspect of this failure lies in the inability of so many dwellings in these settings to provide what Yancey (1971) and Newman (1973) have termed 'defensible space': the ability of residents to regulate who approaches their homes. Where this is lacking, Newman reports that crime rates are higher. Stollard (1991) provides practical guidance for architects, planners and housing managers in how to use good design in new housing estates and in improving existing estates, to reduce and prevent crime.

Coleman (1985) in her investigation of over 4000 blocks of flats and over 4000 houses, goes into immense detail. Windows and doors should be designed so that visitors can easily be monitored, and each front door should also be overlooked by a neighbour. Fences and gates should provide a buffer zone between the home and the outside world. Back gardens should provide security against intruders, and privacy. Garages should be under the visual control of people in the house and thus more secure against crime.

She also makes a series of suggestions referring to the design or adaptation of blocks of flats and estates, in order that residents have a greater control over who enters the semi-public area around the blocks. She points out that design failure may go further, to contaminate the next generation: if parents have been reared in flats themselves, without an appreciation of the need to care for their own domestic environment, their children may grow up doubly disadvantaged, and fail to care themselves in their turn. Her ideas have been put into practice, with mixed results (Morris and Winn, 1990; Lowry, 1991).

4.4 ASSOCIATION OF HOUSING AND POVERTY

The effect of poverty on health has been noted many times in these pages. It remains only to point out that the continuing links tend to show up, in contemporary Britain, through illness, especially serious and chronic illnesses which threaten the quality of life, and different patterns of mortality. The reason differences persist are, Wilkinson (1991) argues, due to relative differences:

> Once countries have reached the standards of affluence of the developed world, further increases in ABSOLUTE income cease to matter very much [to measures of health] . . . what now matters in rich countries is RELATIVE income.

It is the relative egalitarianism of increasing wealth in countries like Japan that has accounted for its rising life expectancy, according to Wilkinson, while Britain has remained relatively stagnant: death rates for young adults in Britain have actually been rising, a trend which cannot be attributed to AIDS alone, and class differences in health show extraordinary persistence. It is a truism that wealth does not guarantee health. One sign that is routinely quoted as an index of growing affluence is that of the decreasing size of households. It is extremely common to find couples or solitary individuals living in dwellings that in previous generations would have housed large boisterous families. This may be an indication that, as well as becoming richer, we are finding it harder to get along with one another. What sort of a society will it be when there are fewer than 2 inhabitants in each house, and 50% of the population live on their own?

4.5 HOUSING FOR DISADVANTAGED GROUPS

One attempt to bring a greater sense of justice and fairness into the housing market has been, via state or philanthropic initiatives, by introducing housing opportunities available only to those identified as disadvantaged. Council housing, for long available only to 'the working classes' is the most important British example. Now council housing managers have been put into an impossible dilemma, as intending tenants in the greatest need (the homeless) compete with those for whom the system was originally created: ordinary working-class families. There are surrealist dilemmas too: local authorities who evict a tenant may immediately be obliged to rehouse him or her on the grounds of homelessness.

In a housing market where demand for decent rented homes exceeds their supply, housing authorities have to make difficult (and politically potentially dangerous) decisions every single day. As medical workers have become involved in this process, they share the risk, discomfort and confusion. Some consider they should withdraw altogether from such work.

The pool of available council homes has shrunk as many have been sold off, and councils effectively barred from building replacements. At the same time, central government policy has been to shift the task of caring for vulnerable groups – the frail elderly, the mentally ill, those with learning disabilities – from the National Health Service to local authorities. These groups appear certain to increase in size, as the hospitals run down and old people live longer. Despite the expression of much worthy sentiment, there is little evidence that sufficient links are yet forged between the two groups of authorities to provide an adequate and appropriate supply of housing, which must certainly be the key resource for their care.

In the Third World too, targeting the most vulnerable and poorest groups may be a major problem for health service planners. Wealth inequalities in Third World cities are enormous, with equivalent consequences for health. Harpham *et al.* (1988, Chapter 4) give a succinct description of many of these problems. The growth of an affluent section of the population may encourage the growth of health services based on ability to pay, thus reducing the health resources available to the poor. Deciding who are the poorest, and what precisely are their needs, may turn out to be rather more difficult than appearances suggest: the residents in poor areas need to be involved themselves in decisions affecting their well-being, and their enthusiastic participation cannot be taken for granted.

4.6 BLURRING DISTINCTIONS BETWEEN OWNERS AND RENTERS

Modern industrial society is increasingly diversified. In housing terms the major distinction is between owners and renters, but this is beginning to break down. Initially housing interests were divided between a small group of owners and landlords and a much larger group of tenants. State agencies acting as landlords blunted the vulnerability of some tenants to market forces. However, state agencies (or any other landlords) may fail if they do not harness the co-operative energies of their tenants.

Increasingly, governments are encouraging alternatives to the landlord–tenant relationship based solely on the cash nexus. This is happening in three ways: granting more control over their environment to tenants; creating new forms of renting, via organizations such as housing associations and co-operatives; and opening up methods of purchase that stop short of total ownership.

4.6.1 INCREASING TENANT CONTROL

There are now numerous examples of self-help movements among local groups of local authority tenants who are organizing to defend their own interests and achieve control over the environment around their own homes. The way this has happened in Divis flats, Belfast, has already been mentioned, as it is recounted by Sluka (1989) and Lowry (1991). Lowry also describes the action taken by residents of the Easthall estate in Glasgow when faced with huge bills for heating their poorly-built homes. A long publicity campaign by the tenants against their landlord, the Housing Department of Glasgow District Council, eventually brought the promise to provide some new homes. A successful example from Liverpool is described on p. 96.

Some of the examples of shanty-town development from the Third World are even more graphic. In San Martin, on the edge of Buenos Aires, government attempts to raze the settlement were resisted, largely by women and children who stood in the way of the bulldozers; eventually the residents themselves built a health centre (Hardoy *et al.*, 1990, Chapter 2). No doubt many similar stories could be amassed from around the world, less dramatic in detail perhaps but similarly indicative of the capacity of poor people for self-help.

4.6.2 HOUSING ASSOCIATIONS AND CO-OPERATIVES

While much attention in Britain in the last decade has focused on government efforts to sell council housing to its tenants (and to others) a new force in housing, the housing association movement, has been making great progress, providing a variety of renting arrangements which offer alternatives to existing forms of tenure. Some schemes are deliberately aimed at categories of disadvantaged individuals or households, and can offer them either a temporary breathing space before they pass the hurdles of entry into a major tenure, or a permanent home. Housing associations as yet provide for too small a share of the housing market for their impact on health to be quantified, but they appear to offer a positive and valuable option for a substantial number of people.

Eldon Street, Vauxhall, Liverpool

Eldon Street is half a mile from Liverpool City Centre in the heart of Liverpool's dockland. Many of its original population were moved out of slum housing into suburban estates and in 1978 the city council decided without consultation to demolish the rest. Local people resisted, forming the Eldon Street Community Association, conducting their own survey of people's housing wishes and striving to building housing co-operatives.

Despite enormous continuing social and economic problems (adult male unemployment exceeded 50% at one time) the Eldon Street Community Association succeed over 10 years in building the largest housing co-operative in the country and developed community businesses and social care networks. Local building and land which becomes derelict are assessed as community resources. New ways of working with professionals from outside the area have increased the power and self-esteem of local people. The professionals have learned something, too.

Source: Ashton and Seymour (1988) pp. 107–9.

4.6.3 ALTERNATIVE FORMS OF OWNERSHIP

Most people who buy their home can do so only if they first raise a mortgage. Schemes to make owner-occupation possible for a wider section of the population, such as splitting the purchase (and the equity in the property) between an individual and a financial institution, are in their relative infancy, but may also contribute to reducing the differences in wealth, power and probably health, between owners and renters.

4.7 GROWING AWARENESS OF HEALTH ISSUES IN HOUSING

Signs of an increasing acceptance of the health consequences of housing have come from local authorities in recent years. Many have restricted the movements of young families into tower blocks. The courts have underlined their responsibilities towards their tenants' health: in 1990 a boy of 5 was awarded £12 000 compensation for aggravation of his asthma caused by living in a damp council flat in Peckham, South London.

There is growing evidence too from among council tenants of the health consequences of poor housing. When nearly a thousand residents of a poor council estate in Bristol were asked 'What do you think would improve your health or the health of those who live with you?' the commonest replies were 'Better housing' (30%) or a 'A better environment' (15%) (Main and Main, 1990). Strenuous efforts to promote preventive health care by a primary health care team on another severely deprived council estate, this time in Stockton-on-Tees, appear to have been very successful, although additional clerical staff were needed to cope with the work (Marsh and Channing, 1988).

Such initiatives are especially welcome in that they may have to overcome blinkered views and established prejudice, among the very people who stand to gain most from them. Calnan (1987) for instance, reports a small group of working-class informants who stubbornly refuse to accept the findings of the Black Report. And Cornwell (1984) finds no shortage of opinion from among her East London families that not only does wealth have nothing to do with health, but an almost universal agreement that smoking does not cause lung cancer.

4.8 CHANGING ROLE OF PUBLIC HEALTH AGENCIES

In Chapter 1 of this book, the growing awareness of the need for official regulation of housing was charted. This was not achieved without dissenting voices: as an opponent to the Torrens Act, 1867 stated, 'If we provide housing for the poor, the next demand might be to provide clothing if not carriages and horses'. Some measures, such as the ticketing of houses in Glasgow to prevent overcrowding, concerned what went on inside the dwelling: the idea of an English (or a Scot's) home as a castle, impregnable to outsiders, has been repeatedly compromised.

Housing legislation designed to improve the lives of poor people has resulted in a degree of control being exercised over them: in White's (1986) phrase, there has been 'no end to the number of officials' whose job was to tell them how to live their lives. The rise of public health agencies has been at a cost to individual freedom, and often it has been the poor who have paid more than their share of that price.

An example of a contemporary dilemma concerns the need to protect children and women from the men they share their lives and homes with. For a hundred children a year, home is not so much where they live as where they die, victims of parental violence. Many more women are driven out of their homes. Public opinion is still cautious and begrudging in its support for those state servants who seek to prevent or minimize this evil. Health and welfare workers need to tread carefully once they cross domestic thresholds.

In the wider context there are positive signs. 'Community Medicine' is giving way to 'Public Health'. This change in nomenclature suggests a shift in medical and political circles from a concentration in the treatment of individual cases towards concern with health promotion and Green issues, 'looking after the things that look after us'. Ashton (1991) notes that this involves re-examining housing with 'ecological eyes'.

Public Health Departments of Health Authorities are now obliged to produce an Annual Report which highlights topics of current concern to the health of local populations. Directors of Public Health are clearly key figures in these changing functions, and 89% of them replied to a questionnaire on the subject of housing in late 1989 (Roderick *et al.*, 1991).

One in three thought that housing constituted a major health problem in their district. Not surprisingly, those in cities (especially inner cities) were more likely to think this was the case. Nearly half altogether felt that housing was perceived generally to be a problem in their district. Poor housing conditions, and a lack of housing for those with special needs, were seen as the commonest kinds of housing difficulties.

In just over half of the districts, a member of the Department of Public Health Medicine spent time on housing issues, usually on a regular basis. In the great majority of instances, this concerned allocating medical priority in rehousing cases. Participation in other issues was not commonly reported. Joint care planning with local authorities relevant to housing, for example, was carried out in only 15 districts, only 8% of the sample. Over half had included housing matters in their current report, and others said they intended to do so in the future. Lack of time, manpower, or information was frequently cited as the reason it had not been done. However, only a minority of Public Health Departments actually had links with local housing organizations, and this usually concerned the provision of housing to groups with special needs.

There are grounds for optimism at the highest level too. Arising out of the earlier 'Health For All by 2000' movement, the World Health Organisation has promoted a 'Healthy Cities Project' since 1985. Its idea has been to encourage practical models of health promotion at city level, and well over 100 cities have become involved. WHO acts as a catalyst, setting new agendas for health, raising public awareness of health issues, and establishing models of good practice. Such grandiose ideas clearly take some time to filter down to the local level, but in their review of progress Ashton and Seymour (1988) conclude, 'The importance of the project has been to assert the need to think globally and act locally in the first instance'. It remains to be seen how much remains pious words, and how much concerted and effective action which will lead to improvements in housing and health.

References and further reading

FURTHER READING

Chapter 1 draws in particular on a number of key sources. These are, covering the period up to World War I, the two masterworks of Anthony S. Wohl, *The Eternal Slum: Housing and Social Policy in Victorian London* (1977) and *Endangered Lives: Public Health in Victorian Britain* (1983). John Burnett's *A Social History of Housing 1815–1985* (2nd edn, 1986) is an excellent straightforward account of the housing side of the relationship for the whole period of study covered here. Jerry White's reconstructions of particular locations, *Rothschild Buildings: Life in an East End tenement block 1887–1920* (1980) and *The Worst Street in North London: Campbell Bunk, Islington, between the Wars* (1986) are models of their kind, and will be of interest to the scholar and the general reader alike. We need many more of these kinds of enquiries.

Some of the topics in Chapter 2 have been discussed previously by Stella Lowry in her book, *Housing and Health* (1990). Much of this material appeared previously in the *British Medical Journal*. An influential (and controversial) study of the influence of the built environment on behaviour is Alice Coleman's *Utopia on Trial: Vision and Reality in Planned Housing* (1985). A useful summary of a great deal of research, plus an extensive bibliography, is to be found in Susan J. Smith's *Housing and Health: a review and research agenda* (1989).

Defying easy categorization, Witold Rybczynski's *Home: a short history of an idea* (1988) is an extremely stimulating discussion of a concept which has been largely neglected by writers on health.

I have paid regrettably little attention to the relationship between homes and health outside the UK, principally due to the difficulties of obtaining source material. Ann-Louise Shapiro's *Housing the Poor of Paris 1850–1902* (1985) permits fascinating comparisons to be made with the British experience, but international comparison is another area where further work is needed. Forthcoming developments in Eastern Europe will certainly be worth watching.

The huge question of the health consequences of housing in the Third World, especially in its cities, deserves several volumes, but T. Harpham *et al.*'s *In the Shadow of the City: Community Health and the Urban Poor* (1988) and J. E. Hardoy *et al.*'s *The Poor Die Young: Housing and Health in Third World Cities* (1990) make an encouraging start.

REFERENCES

Acheson, E.D. (1990) Edwin Chadwick and the World we Live in. *The Lancet*, **336**, 8729, 15 December 1482–5.

Allen, G. and Crow, G. (eds.) (1989) *Home and Family: Creating the Domestic Sphere*, Macmillan, Basingstoke.

Amis, P. and Lloyd. P. (eds.) (1990) *Housing Africa's Urban Poor*, Manchester University Press, Manchester.

Ash, J. (1980) The rise and fall of high-rise housing in England, in *The Consumer Experience of Housing* (eds. C. Ungerson and V. Karn) Gower, London, 93–123.

Ashton, J. (1991) Sanitarian becomes ecologist: the new environmental health. *Br. Med. J.*, **302**, 189–90.

Ashton, J. and Seymour, H. (1988) *The New Public Health*, Open University Press, Milton Keynes.

Audit Commission (1991) *Healthy Housing: the role of the environmental health officer*, HMSO, London.

Bagley, C. (1974) The built environment as an influence on personality and social behaviour: a spatial study, in *Psychology and the Built Environment* (eds. D. Canter and T.R. Lee), Architectural Press, London, 156–62.

Bain, D.J.G. and Philip, A.E. (1975) Going to the doctor: attendances by members of 100 families in their first year in a new town. *JRCGP*, **25**, 821–7.

Barker D.J.P. *et al.* (1990) Poor housing in childhood and high rates of stomach cancer in England and Wales. *B.J. Cancer*, **61**, 575–8.

Beresford, M.W. (1971) The Back to Back House in Leeds 1787–1837, in *The History of the Working Class Housing: a symposium* (ed. S.D. Chapman), David and Charles, Newton Abbott, pp. 93–132.

Bhopal, R.S. *et al.* (1991) Proximity of the home to a cooling tower and risk of non-outbreak Legionnaires disease. *Br. Med. J*, **302**, 378–83.

Birtchnell, J., Masters, N. and Deahl, M. (1988) Depression and the Physical Environment: a study of young married women on a London Housing Estate. *Br. J. Psychiatry*, **153**, 56–64.

Blackman, T. *et al.* (1989) Housing and health: a case study of two areas in West Belfast. *J. Soc. Policy*, **18**(1), 1–26.

Booth, T., Simons, K. and Booth, W. (1990) *Outward Bound: relocation and community care for people with learning difficulties*, Open University Press, Milton Keynes.

Bromley, R. (1979) Households suited to high flats. *Town and Country Planning*, **48**(4), 116–18.

Burnett, J. (1986) *A Social History of Housing 1815–1985*, 2nd edn, Methuen, London.

Butt, J. (1971) Working-class housing in Glasgow 1851–1914, in *The History of the Working Class Housing: a symposium* (ed. S.D. Chapman), David and Charles, Newton Abbott, pp. 55–92.

Byrne D.S. *et al.*, (1986) *Housing and Health: the relationship between housing conditions and the health of council tenants*, Gower, London.

Calnan, M. (1987) *Health and Illness: the Lay Perspective*, Tavistock, London.

Chapman, S.D. (ed.) (1971) *The History of the Working Class Housing: a symposium*, David and Charles, Newton Abbott.

Chiu, L.P.W. (1988) Do weather, day of the week and address affect the rate of attempted suicide in Hong Kong? *Social Psychiatry and Psychiatric Epidemiology*, **23**(4), 229–35.

Churchman, A. and Ginsberg, Y. (1984) The image and experience of high-rise housing in Israel. *J. Environmental Psychology*, **4**, 27–41.

Coleman, A. (1985) *Utopia on Trial: Vision and Reality in Planned Housing*, Hilary Shipman, London.

Coleman, M. and Beral, V. (1988) A Review of epidemiological studies of the health effects of living near or working with electricity generation and transmission equipment. *Int. J. Epidemiology*, **17**(1), 1–13.

Connelly, J., Roderick, P. and Victor, C. (1990) Health service planning for the homelessness population: availability and quality of existing information. *Public Health*, **104**, 109–16.

Conway, J. (ed.) (1988) *Prescription for Poor Health: the health crisis for homeless families*, London Food Commission, Maternity Alliance, SHAC and Shelter, London.

Cornwell, J. (1984) *Hard-earned Lives: Accounts of Health and Illness in East London*, Tavistock, London.

Crowther, M.A. (1981) *The Workhouse System 1844–1929*, Batsford, London.

Cullingworth, J.B. (1960) *Housing Needs and Planning Policy*, Routledge, London.

Cullingworth, J.B. *et al.* (1969) *Council Housing: Purposes, Procedures and Priorities*, HMSO, London.

Darley, G. (1978) *Villages of Vision*, Granada, London.

Dear, M.J. and Wolch, J.R. (1987) *Landscapes of Despair: from deinstitutionalization to homelessness*, Polity, Cambridge.

Defoe, D. (1971) *A Tour through the Whole Island of Great Britain 1724–6*, Penguin, Harmondsworth.

Department of the Environment (1972) *The Estate Outside the Dwelling*, HMSO, London.

Department of the Environment (1975) *Social Effects of Living Off the Ground*, Housing Development Directorate Paper 1/75, HMSO, London.

Doggett, M.A. (1989) A Review of the Literature on primary Health Care for Single Homeless People, in *Health Care for Single Homeless People* (eds. S. Williams and I. Allen), Policy Studies Institute, , pp. 321–61.

Dunleavy, P. (1981) *The Politics of Mass Housing in Britain 1945–1975*, Clarendon, Oxford.

Durward, L. (ed.) (1990) *Traveller mothers and babies: who cares for their health?* Maternity Alliance, London.

Dyos, H. J. (1982) *Exploring the Urban Past*, Cambridge University Press, Cambridge.

Elton, P.J. and Packer, J.M. (1987) Neurotic Illness as Grounds for Medical Priority for Rehousing. *Public Health*, **101**, 233–42.

Fanning, D.M. (1967) Families in flats. *Br. Med. J.*, **iv**, 382–6.

Faris, R.E.L. and Dunham, H.W. (1939) *Mental Disorders in Urban Areas*, University of Chicago Press, Chicago.

Farquhar, D.L. (1990) Problems caused by selection criteria in sheltered housing. *Geriatric Medicine*, March, 26.

Feder, G. (1989) Travellers, gypsies and primary care. *J. Coll. Gen. Pract.*, **39**, 425–9.

Fogelman, K., Fox, A.J. and Power, C. (1989) Class and tenure mobility: do they explain social inequalities in Britain? in *Health Inequalities in European countries* (ed. J. Fox), Gower, London, pp. 333–352.

Freedman, J. (1975) *Crowding and Behaviour: the psychology of high density housing*, Freeman, San Francisco.

Freeman, H.L. (ed.) (1984) *Mental Health and the Environment*, Churchill Livingstone, London.

Fried, M. (1963) Grieving for a lost home, in *The Urban Condition* (ed. L.J. Duhl), Basic Books, New York.

Gabe, J. and Williams, P. (1987) Women, housing and mental health. *I.J. Health Services*, **17**, 667–79.

Gans, H. (1967) *The Levittowners*, Allen Lane, London.

Gauldie, E. (1974) *Cruel Habitations: a history of working-class housing 1780–1918*, Allen and Unwin, London.

Gibbons, J.S. and Butler, J.P. (1987) Quality of life of 'new' longstay psychiatric patients: the effects of moving to a hostel. *Br. J. Psychiatry*, **151**, 347–54.

Gillis, A.R. (1977) High-rise housing and psychological strain. *J. Health Soc. Behaviour*, **18**, 418–34.

Gittus, E. (1976) *Flats, Families and Under-fives*, Routledge and Kegan Paul, London.

Godlee, F. (1992) Noise: breaking the silence. *Br. Med. J.*, **304**, 110–13.

Goodman, M. and Crombie, D.L. (1982) Reported illness and change of residence. *JRCGP*, **32**, 609–13.

Hannay, D.R. (1979) *The Symptom Iceberg: A study of Community Health*, Routledge and Kegan Paul, London.

Hannay, D.R. (1981) Mental health and high flats. *J. Chronic Diseases*, **34**, 431–2.

Hannay, D.R. (1984) Mental Health and Symptom Referral in a City, in *Mental Health and the Environment* (ed. H. Freeman), Churchill Livingstone, London, pp. 411–24.

Hardman, R.A. (1965) A comparison of morbidity in two areas. *J. Coll. Gen, Pract.*, **9**, 226–40.

Hardoy, J.E. *et al.* (1990) *The Poor Die Young: Housing and Health in Third World Cities*, Earthscan, London.

Hare, E.H. and Shaw, G.K. (1965) *Mental Health on a New Housing Estate*, Oxford University Press, Oxford.

Harpham, T., Lusty, T. and Vaughan, P. (eds.) (1988) *In the Shadow of the City: Community Health and the Urban Poor*, Oxford University Press, Oxford.

Harrington, M. (1965) Resettlement and self-image. *Human Relations*, **18**(2), 115–37.

Harrison, P. (1985) *Inside the Inner City*, revised edn, Penguin, Harmondsworth.

Hatch, S. and Nissel, C. (1989) *Is Community Care Working? Report on a survey of psychiatric patients discharged into Westminster*, Westminster Association for Mental Health, London.

Hazarika, S. (1987) *Bhopal: Lessons of a Tragedy*, Penguin, New Delhi.

Heller, T. (1982) The effects of involuntary residential location: a review. *Am. J. Com. Psychology*, **10**(4), 471–92.

Hibbitt, E. (1990) Health Promotion with homeless families; extending the role of the midwife. *MCNN*, January, 8–10.

Hooper D. and Ineichen, B. (1979) Adjustment to moving: a follow-up study of the mental health of young families in new housing. *Social Science and Medicine*, **13D**, 163–8.

Hooper, D. *et al.* (1978) Social work intervention on a new housing estate, *BJ Social Work*, **8**(4), 453–64.

Hyndman, S.J. (1990) Housing dampness and health among British Bengalis in East London, *Soc. Sci. Med.*, **30**(1), 131–41.

Ineichen, B. (1973) Housing Classes and Housing Careers: Population Mobility in a redeveloped central urban area. *Social and Economic Administration*, **7**(1), 30–8.

Ineichen, B. (1990) The extent of dementia among old people in residential care. *Int. J. Geriatric Psychiatry*, **5**, 327–35.

Ineichen, B. and Hooper, D. (1974) Wives' mental health and children's behaviour problems in contrasting residential areas. *Social Science and Medicine*, **8**, 369–74.

Jackson, A.A. (1973) *Semi-detached London: Suburban development, life and transport 1900–1939*, Allen and Unwin, London.

James, A. (1991) Homeless women in London: the hostel perspective. *Health Trends*, **23**(2), 80–3.

Jenkins, L. (1991) Refurbished towers of terror handed over to residents, *The Times*, September 28.

Jephcott, P. (1971) *Homes in High Flats*, Oliver and Boyd, Edinburgh.

Jones, K. (1985) *After Hospital: a study of long-term psychiatric patients in York*, University of York, York.

Joseph, P.L.A. *et al.* (1990) A psychiatric clinic for the single homeless in a primary care setting in inner London. *Psychiatric Bulletin*, **14**, 270–1.

Kantor, M.B. (1969) Internal Migration and Mental Illness, in *Changing Perspectives in Mental Illness* (eds. S.G. Plog and R.B. Edgerton) Holt, Rinehart and Winston, New York, pp. 364–94.

Keeley, D.J., Neill, P. and Gallivan, S. (1991) Comparison of the prevalence of reversible airways obstruction in rural and urban Zimbabwean children. *Thorax*, **46**, 549–553.

Key, W.H. (1967) *When People are Forced to Move*, Menninger Foundation, Topeka, KAN.

Kingdon, D. (1991) Homeless and mentally ill. *Health Trends*, **23**(2), 48.

Kogevinas, M. (1990) *Social-demographic differences in cancer survival 1971–83*, HMSO, London.

Langenbach, R.R. (1984) Continuity and Sense of Place: the importance of the symbolic image, in *Mental Health and the Environment* (ed. H.L. Freeman), Churchill Livingstone, London, pp. 455–69.

Lewis, J. (1991) The origins and development of public health in the UK, in *Oxford Textbook of Public Health, vol 1, Influences of Public Health*, 2nd ed (eds. W.W. Holland *et al.*), Oxford University Press, 23–34.

Littlewood, J. and Tinker, A. (1981) *Families in Flats*, HMSO, London.

Lowry, S. (1991) *Housing and Health*, British Medical Journal, London.

MacDonald, J.B. *et al.* (1991) A comparison of the health and functional capacity of tenants within sheltered and amenity housing in Scotland. *J. Clin. Exp. Gerontology*, **13**(3), 173–87.

McCarthy, P., Byrne, D., Harrison, S. and Keithley, J. (1985) Housing type, housing location and mental health. *Social Psychiatry*, **20**, 125–30.

McNally, C.E. (1935) *Public Ill-Health*, Gollancz, London.

Main, J.A. and Main P.G.N. (1990) The Black Report (letter). *Br. Med. J.*, **301**, 608.

Marmot, A.F. (1983) Flats fit for families: an evaluation of post-occupancy evaluation. *Design Studies*, **4**(2), 92–9.

Marsh, G.N. and Channing, D.M. (1988) Narrowing the health gap between a deprived and an endowed community. *Br. Med. J.* **296**, 173–6.

Marshall, M. (1989) Collected and neglected: are Oxford hostels for the homeless filling up with disabled psychiatric patients? *Br. Med. J.*, **299**, 706–9.

Marshall, M. and Gath, D. (1992) What happens to homeless mentally ill people? Follow up of residents of Oxford hostels for the homeless. *Br. Med. J.*, **304**, 79–80.

Martin, E.M. *et al.* (1957) Incidence of Neurosis in a new housing estate. *Br. J. Prev. Soc. Med.*, **11**, 196–202.

M'Gonigle, G.C.M. and Kirby, J. (1936) *Poverty and Public Health*, Gollancz, London.

Mitchell, R.E. (1971) Some social implications of high density. *Am. Soc. Review*, **36**, 18–29.

Moore, N.C. (1974) Psychiatric illness and living in flats. *Br. J. Psychiatry*, **125**, 500–7.

Moore, N.C. (1975) Social aspects of flat dwellers. *Public Health*, **89**, 109–15.

Moore, N.C. (1976) The personality and mental health of flat dwellers. *Br. J. Psychiatry*, **128**, 259–61.

Morris, J. (1991) *Camden Living Options Review*, London Borough of Camden, London.

Morris, J. and Winn, M. (1990) *Housing and Social Inequality*, Hilary Shipman, London.

Moser, K.A., Pugh, H.S. and Goldblatt, P.O. (1988) Inequalities in Women's Health: looking at mortality differentials using an alternative approach. *Br. Med. J.*, **296**, 1221–4.

National Consumer Council (1991) *Death-trap Housing*, London.

Newman, O. (1973) *Defensible Space*, Architectural Press, London.

Nuttgens, P. (1989) *The Home Front: Housing the People 1840–1990*, BBC Books, London.

Oliver, P. *et al.* (1981) *Dunroamin: The Suburban Semi and its Enemies*, Barrie and Jenkins, London.

Pahl, J. and Vaile, M. (1988) Health and health care among travellers. *J. Social Policy*, **17**(2) 195–213.

Parsons, L. (1987) Medical Priority for Rehousing. *Public Health*, **101**(6), 435–41.

Paterson, C.M. and Roderick, P. (1990) Obstetric Outcome in Homeless Women. *Br. Med. J.* **301**, 263–6.

Payne, S. (1991) *Women, Health and Poverty*, Harvester Wheatsheaf, Hemel Hempstead.

Perry, S. and Pearl, L. (1988) Power frequency magnetic field and illness in multi-storey blocks. *Public Health*, **102**, 11–18.

Price, J.A. *et al.* (1990) Measurement of airborne mite antigen in homes of asthmatic children. *Lancet*, **336** (8720), 895–7.

Pritchett, V.S. (1968) *A Cab at the Door*, Chatto and Windus, London.

Reichenheim, M.E. and Harpham, T. (1991) Maternal Mental Health in a squatter settlement in Rio de Janeiro. *Br. J. Psychiatry*, **159**, 683–90.

Reynolds, I. and Nicholson, C. (1969) Living off the ground. *Architects Journal*, **34**, 150–4.

Richards, L. (1990) *Nobody's Home*, Oxford University Press, Oxford.

Richman, N. (1974) Effects of housing on preschool mothers and their children. *Dev. Med. Child Neurology*, **16**, 53–8.

Roderick, P., Victor, C. and Connelly, J. (1991) Is housing a public health issue? *Br. Med. J.*, **302**, 157–60.

Rosen, G. (1973) Disease, Debility and Death, in *The Victorian City: images and Realities, Vol 2* (eds. H.J. Dyos and M. Wolff), Routledge and Kegan Paul, London, pp. 625–69.

Rybczynski, W. (1988) *Home: a short history of an idea*, Heinemann, London.

Shanks, N.J. (1988) Medical morbidity of the homeless. *J. Epidemiology and Com. Health*, **42**, 183–6.

Shapiro, A-L. (1985) *Housing the Poor of Paris 1850–1902*, University of Wisconsin Press.

Sluka, J.A. (1989) Living on their nerves: nervous debility in Northern Ireland, *Health Care for Women International*, **10**, 2–3. Reprinted in Davis, D. and Low, S. (1990) *Gender, Health and Illness: the case of nerves*, Hemisphere, London.

Smith, R. (1974) Multi-dwelling building in Scotland 1750–1970: a study based on housing in the Clyde Valley in A Sutcliffe, *Multi-storey Living: the British Working-Class Experience*, Croom Helm, London, 207–43.

Smith, S.J. (1989) *Housing and Health: a review and research agenda*, Centre for Housing Research, University of Glasgow.

Smith, S.J. (1990) Aids, Housing and Health. *Br. Med. J.*, **300**, 243–4.

Stephens, B., Mason, J.P. and Isely, R.B. (1985) Health and low-cost housing. *World Health Forum*, **6**, 59–62.

Stevenson, J. (1977) *Social Conditions in Britain Between the Wars*, Penguin, Harmondsworth.

Stokols, D. and Shumaker, S. (1982) The psychological context of residential mobility and well-being. *J. Social Issues*, **38**, 149–71.

Stollard, P. (ed.) (1991) *Crime Prevention Through House Design*, E&FN Spon, London.

Strachan, D.P. (1991) Damp housing, mould, allergy, and childhood asthma. *Proc. R. Coll. Physicians of Edinburgh*, **21**, 140–6.

Sutherland, I. (1986) Happy in the Highrise. *New Society*, **78**(1245), 22.

Sutton, M. (1988) Personal communication.

Taylor, I.C. (1974) The Insanitary Housing Question and tenement dwellings in nineteenth century Liverpool, in *Multi-storey Living: the British Working Class Experience* (ed. A. Sutcliffe), Croom Helm, London, 41–87.

Taylor, S. (1938) Suburban Neurosis. *The Lancet*, **i**, 759–61.

Taylor, Lord and Chave, S. (1964) *Mental Health and the Environment*, Longman, London.

Teeson, M. and Buhrich, N. (1990) Prevalence of schizophrenia in a refuge for homeless men: a five year follow-up. *Psychiatric Bulletin*, **14**, 597–600.

Thornicroft, G. (1991) Social deprivation and rates of treated mental disorder: developing statistical models to predict psychiatric service utilization. *Br. J. Psychiatry*, **158**, 475–84.

Thorpe, F.T. (1939) Demolition Melancholia. *Br. Med. J.* **2**, 127–8.

Timms, P.W. and Fry A.H. (1989) Homelessness and mental illness. *Health Trends*, **21**, 70–1.

Tinker, A. (1991) Granny flats: the British experience. *J. Housing for the Elderly*, **7**(2), 41–53.

Toon, P.D. *et al.* (1987) Audit of work at a medical centre for the homeless over one year. *J.R. Coll. Gen. Pract.*, **37**, 120–2.

Townsend, P. and Davidson, N. (1982) *Inequalities in Health: the Black Report*, Penguin, Harmondsworth.

Treble, J.H. (1971) Liverpool working-class housing 1801–1851, in *The History of the Working Class Housing: a symposium* (ed. S.D. Chapman), David and Charles, Newton Abbott, pp. 163–220.

Van Vliet, W. (1983) Families in apartment buildings: sad storeys for children? *Environment and Behaviour*, **15**(2), 211–34.

Vassilas, C. and Cook, D. (1990) Registration among the homeless in an inner city practice. *Health Trends*, **22**(2), 89–90.

Victor, C.R., Connelly J., Roderick P. and Cohen, C. (1989) Use of hospital services by homeless families in an inner London health district. *Br. Med. J.* **299**, 725–7.

Webster, P. (1983) A Community growing from the rubble. *The Guardian*, 5 Sept.

Webster, C. (1990) *The Victorian Public Health Legacy: a challenge to the future*, Public Health Alliance,

Weller, M.P.I. (1989) Mental Illness: Who Cares? *Nature*, **339**, 249–52.

Weller, B.G.A. *et al.* (1987) Crisis at Christmas 1986. *Lancet*, **i**, 553–4.

White, J. (1980) *Rothschild Buildings: Life in a East End Tenement Block 1887–1920*, Routledge, London.

White, J. (1986) *The Worst Street in North London: Campbell Bunk, Islington between the wars*, Routledge, London.

Wilkinson, R. (1991) Inequality is bad for your health. *The Guardian*, 12 June, p. 21.

Williams, S. and Allen, I. (1989) *Health Care for Single Homeless People*, Policy Studies Institute, London.

Williamson, R.C. (1981) Adjustment to the high-rise variables in a German Sample. *Environment and Behaviour*, **13**(3), 289–310.

Wilner, D.M. *et al.* (1962) *Housing, Environment and Family Life*, Johns Hopkins University Press, Baltimore.

Wohl, A.S. (1977) *The Eternal Slum: Housing and Social Policy in Victorian London*, Edward Arnold, London.

Wohl, A.S. (1983) *Endangered Lives: Public Health in Victorian Britain*, Methuen, London.

Worsdall, F. (1989) *The Glasgow Tenement: a way of life*, revised edn, Chambers, Edinburgh.

Yancey, W.L. (1971) Architecture, interaction and social control: the case of a large-scale housing project. *Environment and Behaviour*, **3**(1), 3–21.

Yuchtman-Ya'ar, E., Spiro, S.E. and Ram, J. (1979) Reaction to rehousing; loss of community or frustrated aspirations? *Urban Studies*, **16**, 113–9.

Index